3   45/.

Law in the World Community

The Common Law of Mankind (1958)

Law, Freedom and Welfare (1963)

The Law of International Institutions

The Prospects of International Adjudication (1964)
International Immunities (1961)
The Proper Law of International Organizations (1962)

The Headquarters of International Institutions (1945)

Human Rights and International Labour Standards (1960)

The International Protection of Trade Union Freedom (1957)

Space Law (1965)

Law in
the World Community

C. Wilfred Jenks

LL.D. (Cantab.), Hon. LL.D. (Edinburgh),
of Gray's Inn, Barrister-at-law

Member of the Institute of International Law,
Member of the International Academy of Comparative Law,
Principal Deputy Director-General
of the International Labour Office

Longmans

LONGMANS, GREEN AND CO LTD
48 Grosvenor Street, London W1
*Associated companies, branches and representatives
throughout the world*

*Printed in Great Britain by
The Camelot Press Ltd., London and Southampton*

For
Craig and Bruce
and
their generation

Contents

Acknowledgements   viii

Preface   ix

1   Law in a World of Change: An Agenda for a Dialogue   1
Moscow

2   Universality, Coexistence and the Rule of Law   15
Warsaw

3   Sovereignty Today   31
Athens

4   The New Dimensions of International Law   42
Teheran

5   Law and the Pursuit of Peace   56
New Delhi

6   Mutual Aid in International Law   66
Madras

7   Tolerance and Good-neighbourliness as Concepts of International Law   83
Singapore

8   Freedom under Law in the World Community   94
Tokyo

9   Due Process of Law in International Organisations   103
Addis Ababa

10   Human Rights in a World of Diverse Cultures in the Light of the Spanish Tradition   119
Salamanca

11   The Equality of Man in International Law   134
Washington, D.C.

12   The Open Society and International Law   150
Chicago

Index   161

Acknowledgements

I must acknowledge my indebtedness to all the learned bodies whose kind invitations to address them in the course of my travels prompted the addresses collected in this volume, namely: the Faculty of Law of the Hailé Selassié I University, Addis Ababa; the Panteios School of Political Science, Athens; the Northwestern University School of Law, Chicago; the Indian Society of International Law and the Indian Branch of the International Law Association, New Delhi; the Madras State Unit of the Indian Law Institute, Madras; the Faculty of Law of the University of Moscow; the Faculty of Law of the University of Salamanca; the Faculty of Law of the University of Teheran; the Faculty of Law of the Imperial University of Tokyo; the Institute of Law of the Polish Academy of Sciences, Warsaw; and the Howard University School of Law, Washington, D.C.

For me to mention by name all of the friends, old and new, to whose personal initiative I owe the enviable privilege of these invitations would be so invidious an undertaking that they will, I trust, allow me to thank them in these general terms, which are no less wholehearted because they remain so general. It is a keen pleasure to record my deep appreciation of the warm hospitality and unfailing courtesy with which I was always welcomed and heard. I am particularly appreciative of the complete freedom which I enjoyed everywhere to express fully my views on large questions of policy, involving some of the fundamentals of international law and the progress of international institutions, which my hosts knew must be expected to diverge substantially from their own traditional or current views.

In preparing these addresses for the press I have made some slight additions to the original texts to take account of subsequent developments, and in particular of the approval by the General Assembly of the United Nations of the Covenants on Civil and Political Rights and on Economic, Social and Cultural Rights and of the Treaty on Principles Governing the Activities of States in the Exploration and Use of Outer Space, including the Moon and Other Celestial Bodies, but without anywhere changing the nature or emphasis of the original argument.

C. W. J.

Preface

The place of law in the world community is too large an issue to remain the professional responsibility of lawyers. It is a major challenge to contemporary statesmanship which calls for the broadest understanding throughout the community. It involves a choice between conflicting legal philosophies which has attracted the attention of the whole world in an exceptionally dramatic manner as the result of the equal division of opinion in the International Court of Justice in the *South West Africa Cases*. The choice implies decisions of long-range international policy which affect the peace, freedom and welfare of all mankind.

In the *South West Africa Cases* seven judges (who became a majority by the casting vote of the President) took the view that law can serve social needs 'only through and within the limits of its own discipline'[1] and that the duty of the International Court is 'to apply the law as it finds it, not to make it'.[2] Seven other judges dissented on grounds which one of them expressed as being that the historical development of law is a 'continual process of the cultural enrichment of the legal order by taking into account values or interests which had previously been excluded from the sphere of law'.[3] This sharp division of view reflects the most debated issues of twentieth-century jurisprudence. It is a natural projection of the conflicts of policy and interest which are the warp and woof of contemporary international politics.

International law has been passing in recent years through the most severe crisis of growth in its history. There have been fundamental changes in the political, economic and social structure of the world. The number of independent states has doubled in a generation. There have been dramatic shifts in the distribution of power and influence. The concept of one world and conflicting ideologies and allegiances have been continuously in mortal combat. New economic problems and policies have become a major preoccupation of statesmanship. An increased concern for human rights and social policy has set new sights for political action. The impact of advanced science and technology has created a wide range of ever more baffling problems. There have been

---

[1] 1966 I.C.J., 34. [2] *Ibid.*, 48. [3] *Ibid.*, 252.

ix

far-reaching, but not yet decisive, developments in international organisation. The constant inter-play of the new forces released by these
changes has confronted the contemporary international lawyer with
problems unprecedented in scope, complexity and urgency for which
established precedent affords no sufficient answer.

These problems go far beyond the technicalities of international
law. They involve basic issues of public policy affecting the relationship of law and force in the maintenance of peace, order and good
government, the relationship of law, politics and economics, the
relationship of law, science and technology, and the relationship of
law, morality and humanity. They are a challenge to the community
as a whole.

The theme of the present volume is a reflection of these considerations. The place of law in the world community is not a technical
problem of jurisprudence but a broad issue of public policy. The
creation of a new world of law constitutes a challenge to each
and every part of the world, but the nature of the challenge varies
with differences of tradition, interest, outlook and policy which vary
widely from one country to another. To evolve the consensus necessary
for effective action we must accommodate a wide range of divergent
preoccupations and attitudes and the stakes involved must be assessed
by a more varied company than that of professional international
lawyers.

The present volume is the outcome of an attempt to outline these
issues for the general public which they so vitally concern as
well as for the younger generation of international lawyers who will
be called upon to play so large a part in their solution. It consists of
twelve addresses delivered during the last two years in ten different
countries in four different continents: in Addis Ababa, Athens,
Chicago, Madras, Moscow, New Delhi, Salamanca, Singapore,
Teheran, Tokyo, Warsaw and Washington, D.C. Each address deals
with some aspect of the present crisis of growth in the development of
international law of special concern to the audience which I was
addressing but there is, I trust and believe, a unity of thought and
approach running through the volume as a whole which is of wider and
more permanent interest.

Thus, in Moscow I suggested an agenda for a dispassionate dialogue
concerning the intellectual processes by which we evolve and formulate
principles of law; in Warsaw I discussed some of the intellectual re-
adjustments necessary to permit of coexistence in freedom in a world

which remains profoundly and tragically divided but in which there has nevertheless been an encouraging, though precarious, relaxation of the international tension of the years following the Second World War; in Athens I dealt with the bedevilment of progress towards world order by the concept of sovereignty; in Teheran with the inadequacy of a law 'which altereth not' in a dynamic world shaped by the interplay of law, economics and politics, law, science and technology, and law, humanity and morality; in New Delhi and Madras with the complex interplay of collective security and non-alignment and of international and national responsibility for economic growth; in Singapore with tolerance and good-neighbourliness as concepts of international law and political conditions of any long-term settlement in South-East Asia or adjustment in the relationship between China and the rest of the world; in Tokyo with the conflicting claims of consensus and principle as guides to policy, and the scope and limits of international action to promote freedom and welfare under law; in Addis Ababa with due process of law as a crucial element in international morality, the cornerstone of effective world organisation, and a decisive factor in the future place of Africa in the world community; in Salamanca with the challenge of the Universal Declaration of Human Rights to the best in all our traditions and its significance for the liberalisation of national policies in societies emerging from the grip of authoritarianism; in Washington with the explosive potential of the ideal of the equality of man; and in Chicago with the responsibility in all these matters which falls upon the Western world.

These varied and complex challenges define the dimensions of the task confronting us. Of course we must start with the world as we find it, but the future will nevertheless be in large measure what we make of it. Law is both a reflection of and one of the decisive formative influences of society; it mirrors the past but also projects the future. Law is not the servant of power; it cannot ignore the facts of power, but its mission is to provide a discipline within which power is guided and limited by moral purpose and enlisted in the service of a community devoted to freedom and welfare. Law is but one of the elements of social control; but it is the element which distinguishes a free society from authoritarianism and anarchy.

Such is the spirit in which, pragmatically but boldly, and modestly but with stout resolve, we must labour to clarify and fortify the part which the law can play in the creation of a world community of all mankind. The task is not one for lawyers alone, nor can it be completed during a passing season; it is a challenge to the moral sense, political sophistication, social discipline and intellectual resourcefulness of succeeding generations of citizens, scholars and statesmen.

C. WILFRED JENKS

I

Law in a world of change: an agenda for a dialogue[1]

Ours is a privileged generation. We are entering upon a wholly new age in the history of man, an age without precedent in human experience.

It is an age of political, economic, social, technological and cultural change unprecedented in scale, rhythm and rate of acceleration. Never before has the dynamic growth of society been a factor larger on the world stage than its continuing stability. It is an age of unbounded opportunity. Never before have the resources at man's disposal made it possible for a single generation to transform the life of all mankind more fundamentally than it has been transformed throughout recorded history. It is an age of unparalleled danger. Never before has man had it in his power to destroy in a few minutes all that he has inherited from past generations and all that his own skill and devotion have contributed to enrich that heritage.

These are fundamental changes in man's relationship to the universe. They call for a fundamental rethinking of all our political philosophies, all our economic dogmas and all our legal theories. They present a challenge which transcends all the ideological controversies of the past. None of us can confront the moral challenge of tomorrow with the intellectual baggage of yesterday.

We live in a new world and this new world is one world. It is not one world in the sense that it has achieved, or is likely to achieve, any unity of purpose, ideology or interest. It is one world in the sense that all the leading centres of power and decision in the world are immediately sensitive to happenings in all its parts. It is one world in the sense that irresponsibility in any part of the world is liable to produce disaster throughout the world. A world which has become one in even this limited degree requires a legal system which gives a fuller expression to its growing unity than previous generations have found necessary. It

[1] An address at the Faculty of Law of the University of Moscow, 22 March 1966.

needs, and is gradually evolving, what I have ventured to describe as a
common law of mankind. Such a common law of mankind presupposes
the acceptance by us all, irrespective of differences of ideology or interest,
of a common responsibility for the common peace, a common responsibility for the common welfare, a common respect for the freedom and
dignity of the common man.

My theme today is the challenge to bold and original thought in the
field of international law which this new world presents for us all, the
responsibility which rests upon us all to review constantly the extent to
which our current thinking corresponds to the scale and complexity of
our current problems. As Professor Grigori Tunkin has so wisely said,
we must free legal science 'from dogmatism, from the use of citations
instead of creative legal thought' and recognise that our aim must 'not
only be knowledge of what exists in international law but active participation in changing it'.[1] The momentum of the past gives neither mastery
of the present nor understanding of the future; only a full understanding
of the past and mastery of the present can give momentum for the future.

We must conceive of the law as a discipline and process of orderly and
constructive change, neither a bastion of the past nor a consecration of
the present, either in the world as a whole, or in any particular country
or society. The common law of mankind, as I understand it, is not the
servant of any particular ideology but a code of accepted principles and
agreed procedures within which we can 'practise tolerance and live
together in peace with one another as good neighbours'. It is not the
projection on a world scale of any particular culture, economic order or
legal system but a synthesis of the values, principles and rules common
to all legal systems which seek to serve the peace, freedom and welfare
of the human family by the restraint of arbitrary power.

A changing world, in which the law serves as a discipline and process
of change, presupposes a growing legal system. The fundamental
problem of international law, as of every legal system, is that of how it
grows. This problem of growth is exceptionally acute at a time when the
community of states has doubled its membership in twenty years.
Strategy has become global; economic policy in every type of economic
system has become increasingly concerned with the problem of dynamic
growth; the progress of education and changes in social structure have
quickened throughout the world a wholly new determination to make a
reality of the human rights and fundamental freedoms proclaimed by the

[1] As quoted in E. McWhinney, *Peaceful Coexistence and Soviet–Western
International Law*, A. W. Sythoff, Leiden, 1964, p. 16.

Universal Declaration of Human Rights and the United Nations Covenants on Human Rights; the pressure of population upon resources has become the greatest of the world's problems; the exhaustion and erosion of natural resources and the pollution of natural environment have become acute anxieties of general concern; and nuclear energy, space exploration, the opening up of the ocean depths, developments in electronics and cybernetics, and the progress of molecular biology, have added a wholly new spectrum of interests and responsibilities to the classical preoccupations of the international lawyer.

In this new world of our time not all is new. Many of the fundamentals of peaceful relations among states, including mutual respect for each other's territory, jurisdiction and internal arrangements, remain unchanged. Much of the law as we have inherited it is an expression of these fundamentals and remains valid, in no wise impaired in its authority or social value by the far-reaching changes of our time.

The foundations of the law are still more permanent. We can, and must, distinguish certain ethical pillars on which the whole structure of the law rests and must always rest. For me there are seven such pillars: the unity of mankind, tolerance, the outlawry of violence, good faith, fair play, mutual aid, and the dignity of man. These are not, however, principles of law, but ethical postulates from which the whole legal system is derived. When we proceed from the ethical foundations of the law to the formulation of its rules we are at once confronted with the problem of defining how such rules emerge and crystallise.

The development of legal systems exhibits a perpetual paradox. As a legal system develops, the specific rules for particular cases out of which it grows tend to be generalised into broader principles. As a legal system develops, it tends to become a mass of complex detail obscuring the first principles on which the system is based. Both these apparently contradictory propositions have substantial validity: each of them illuminates a major element in the growth of the law as a continuous interplay of principle and precedent.

Law grows by the continued vitality of custom, the fruitful application of general principles to new situations and problems, the mellowing influence of equity, the impact of adjudication, the effect of legislative acts, and processes of institutional development. All these factors play significant parts in the contemporary reshaping of international law.

It is not surprising that there should have been wide divergencies of view concerning the relative importance and present and future potentialities of these varied influences upon, and processes of growth in, the law. The processes by which law grows and matures have been one of the central problems of legal philosophy for every school of jurisprudence and one of the crucial tests of practical wisdom and effectiveness in every legal system. It is altogether natural that the speculations of international lawyers on these questions should still exhibit a wide range of divergent views.

My thesis today is that progress in these matters calls for a dispassionate dialogue concerning our fundamental processes of thought regarding the concept of law and the manner in which law grows and develops. I would like to suggest for such a dialogue, an annotated agenda, consisting of nine points:

the general concept of law;

the dogma of sovereignty;

the doctrine that States alone can be subjects of international law;

the place of custom in contemporary international law;

the role of general principles in the development of international law;

the role of equity in the development of international law;

the scope for adjudication in the development of international law;

the need for more effective means of international legislation; and

the significance of processes of institutional development for the growth of the law.

The first three of these points, namely the general concept of law, sovereignty, and the subjects of international law, are more general in character than the following six points. I would not expect any full agreement concerning them at an early date, but I believe that some preliminary exchange of views about them is a necessary preparation for detailed examination of the other points. The immediate purpose of such an exchange would be clarification rather than agreement. It is not necessary to resolve these broad questions before the more specific questions can usefully be discussed if the nature and extent of subsisting divergences of view concerning the broader questions are fully understood. My purpose here is to suggest, rather than to initiate, a dialogue on these matters, but the scope of my suggestion will probably be clearer if I proceed to annotate briefly the nine points of my proposed agenda.

Our dialogue must begin with an analysis of the general concept of law. Three elements in the concept are in my judgment of crucial importance for the contemporary development of international law. In one aspect, law is essentially a restraint upon authority rather than the command of authority; its purpose and function is to limit rather than to reinforce political and economic power. In another aspect, much of law is permissive rather than imperative; it does not consist of commands but of rules for securing desired legal consequences, conferring rights, creating obligations, and attaining other legal results. In this aspect law is a positive instrument rather than a negative restraint, but an instrument of cooperation rather than of authority. The third element is that certainty in the law is alien to the function of law in a dynamic society; the life of the law is a constant interaction of factors of stability and factors of change.

Only if our concept of law includes these three elements can we use the law as an effective instrument enabling international society to adopt a more positive approach to its political, economic and social problems, and accomplish its social purposes in a world and age of growing economic, scientific and technological interdependence.

Assuming such a concept of law, what is the relationship of law and sovereignty? The gap between western and Soviet concepts of sovereignty has frequently been described as wide, by western and Soviet writers alike. Where important differences of concept or emphasis exist, there is nothing to be gained by ignoring or underestimating them. But before assuming that the gap is an unbridgeable gulf, we should perhaps examine the facts of the matter. Let us set out a series of propositions concerning sovereignty.

1. Sovereignty may be defined as the right of a state 'freely and at its own discretion to decide its internal and external affairs without violating the rights of other states or the principles and rules of international law'.

2. 'A sovereign State must not in its international relations behave in an arbitrary fashion, without taking account of the generally recognised principles of international law and the international undertakings which it has voluntarily assumed. To do so would mean to violate the principle of the sovereign equality of all the members of the international community. It would undermine the international community and lead to the unlimited rule of force and violence.'

3. 'Entry into an international organisation or the conclusion of a treaty' involves 'certain obligations which are to a certain extent a restriction' on sovereignty.

4. 'The violation or arbitrary unilateral repudiation of freely assumed undertakings cannot be justified by reference to sovereignty.'

B

These four propositions are all quotations from the English edition of the text book on *International Law* of the Institute of Law of the Academy of Sciences of the U.S.S.R., edited by Kojhevnikov. For my part I subscribe to them in full.

They appear to be reducible to two fundamental principles: first, sovereignty is limited by and does not override the law; secondly, sovereignty is an essentially relative concept, subject to a process of constant erosion by the assumption of new obligations. If these principles are acceptable as a point of departure, we can profitably examine their implications throughout the law.

When we have agreed upon these principles we have in effect agreed that the term 'sovereignty' as it is used in international law and international relations has little or no relationship with sovereignty in the etymological sense in which the term was originally used in the days of absolute monarchy. In this context, whether we should retain or abandon the term becomes a matter of practical convenience rather than of fundamental principle. For my part I prefer to abandon it as misleading and because I believe it has a continuing emotional content which is an encumbrance from the past and inhibits us in resolving our present problems on their merits. Biologists teach us that life evolves by the development of simple into more complex organisms. The law and institutions of the world community are evolving in a similar manner and sovereignty is too simple a concept to be helpful in explaining or rationalising the complexities of their contemporary development. The sovereignty of the seas did not survive the work of Grotius. There is no sovereignty in space. International economic life eludes the grasp of sovereignty. The freedom and independence of weak states is protected not by the 'sovereignty' which they are all too apt to regard as the essence of freedom and independence, but by the law which protects them against the rival 'sovereignty' of the strong. Many more examples might be given.

Assuming such a concept of law, and such a view of the relationship of law and sovereignty, who are the subjects of international law? Most of us were still taught a generation ago, and some of us are still taught today, that the only subjects of international law are states. Oppenheim, from whose classical treatise I was taught international law, describes it as 'a law between states only and exclusively'.[1] The Russian textbook on international law to which I have already referred is somewhat less absolute. It says that 'as a rule' only a state can be 'a subject under

[1] Oppenheim, *International Law*, Longmans 1905, p. 341.

present-day international law',[1] but recognises that international organisations are bound by their constitution and that individuals may be
responsible for infringments of international law.[2]

Surely these important qualifications raise a serious doubt whether
the principle itself is satisfactory—does not the whole matter require
review? Are international organisations above the law? If not, they must
be bound by it; if they are bound by it, they are its subjects. If, however,
international organisations have obligations under the law, they must
also have the rights necessary to enable them to discharge these obligations. If they are to operate impartially in a world where the interests of
states conflict, they must have the independence necessary for this
purpose, and the rights necessary to give them such independence.
Again, they must be subjects of the law, in the sense that they have
rights as well as obligations under the law. May it not be that an immense and unnecessary confusion has been introduced into the discussion of the whole subject by failure to appreciate sufficiently clearly that
the legal system of any complex society must necessarily include
widely different types of subject with widely varying rights and
obligations?

The international law of today is, if I may use in a new sense the
expression made so widely familiar in a different context forty years ago
by Korovin, 'the international law of the transition period'.[3] It is the law
of the transition from the anarchy which has characterised international
relations throughout history towards an organised world community.
As such it must show the capacity for adaptation, change and growth
implied in the idea of a transition. We are in process of evolving a
common law of mankind. Such a law must define the rights and obligations of all the constituent elements of the growing world community
from the community itself to the individual human beings who are, as
John Westlake said seventy years ago, its 'ultimate members'.[4] This does
not mean or imply that the world community, the United Nations as the
general international organisation which constitutes the backbone of its
political structure, the world agencies which discharge specialised
responsibilities on behalf of the community, the regional agencies, states,
non-governmental bodies, and individuals have, or can ever have, the

[1] f.I. Kojhevnikov, *ed., International Law.* Institute of Law of the Academy
of Sciences of the U.S.S.R., no date, p. 89.
[2] *Ibid.,* p. 90.
[3] *Mezhdunarodnoe pravo perekhodnogo vremeni,* Moscow, 1923.
[4] Reproduced in J. Westlake, *Collected Papers on Public International Law,*
Cambridge University Press, 1914, p. 78.

8 *Law in the world community*

same relationship, or even similar relationships, to the law, that they participate on the same footing in the creation of rules of law, that the rationale and technique of the manner in which the law becomes binding upon them are identical, or that the rights and obligations which the law extends to them coincide. It does mean that the law embraces them all and defines their mutual rights and obligations in relation to each other; in this sense they are its subjects.

When we have made a preliminary survey of the general concept of law, sovereignty and the subjects of the law, our proposed dialogue should, I submit, come to grips with the metabolism of the law and consider the processes of growth by which the law develops and changes to meet the needs of a dynamic society.

Early law consists primarily of custom but in mature legal systems custom tends to be displaced as an element in the continuing growth of the law by adjudication and legislation. Revolutionary change tends to shake the authority of custom without necessarily providing a satisfactory alternative for it. What stage in the process have we reached in the contemporary development of international law? Is it not true that, as in every legal system, custom does in fact remain, and must remain, a major element of continuing growth until it is effectively replaced by judicial and legislative processes? There is an interesting discussion of the matter in Professor Tunkin's *Droit international public-problèmes théoriques*[1] which for my part I willingly accept as the point of departure of our dialogue.

Two concepts which call for special attention are those of spontaneous custom and institutional custom. Custom creating acts which would formerly have been few in number and spread over long or at least substantial periods of time now follow each other in such repeated instances and quick succession that regularity of conduct can be established in a brief period, while the notoriety of practice necessary to presume general acquiescence in it no longer presupposes any considerable effluxion of time. Hence the concept of spontaneous custom, which can be aptly illustrated by recent developments in the law of the sea and space law; the concept is a necessary adaptation to new and constantly changing technologies. There have been important changes in the method as well as the rate of the formation of custom. As an increasing proportion of the world's business is transacted through international organisations the practice of such organisations takes its place with the practice of states in the accepted body of customary law. Spontaneous

[1] Editions A. Pedone, Paris, 1965, pp. 76-89.

and institutional custom are important illustrations of the continued vitality of custom in contemporary international law.

Custom, even so revitalised by the concepts of spontaneous and institutional custom, provides no immediate answer for the new problem and no answer for the unique case: international law, like every legal system, is constantly confronted with unprecedented situations. It is for this reason that the general principles of law recognised by civilised nations have been so important a factor in the development of international law at every successive stage of its development. The practice of recourse to such principles is no recent innovation. We can trace it back to the international law of the ancient world, in the Middle East and Asia no less than in Europe. The international law of medieval and early modern times was largely a transcription to international relations of Roman law. In the last three centuries the common law of the English speaking world has exercised an influence in the matter comparable to that of the civil law. We have now entered upon a new phase in which the range of legal systems from which international law recruits its principles and rules has become much wider, and embraces the legal systems of a wide diversity of cultural traditions and economic and social structures. I have elsewhere[1] attempted to explore the significance of the shift of emphasis to a world perspective which is indispensable if international law is to continue to find a rich source of further development in the general principles of law recognised by civilised nations. Certainly our perspective must be new and much broader than that of our forefathers or even of our own youth. But while our perspective must be new we cannot, without petrifying the legal system at a stage of development wholly inadequate to contemporary needs, abandon the process of constantly enriching the law by applying old principles to new situations and developing such principles to resolve new problems. The scope which we are prepared to give to the creative genius of the law in drawing upon general principles to respond to the unprecedented challenge of our time is one of the major topics which should be covered in our proposed dispassionate dialogue.

The tempering of the rigour of the law by equity has been a significant feature of the development of mature legal systems. Recourse to equity has likewise been a commonplace of international adjudication since the origins of modern arbitration. Equity is so much more subjective a concept than custom or general principles of law that the definition of its

---

[1] C. W. Jenks, *The Common Law of Mankind.* Stevens and Sons, 1958, pp. 62–172.

role and potentialities presents problems of peculiar difficulty. But the
question should not be excluded from the scope of our proposed
dialogue.

Custom, general principle and equity share a somewhat amorphous
quality. They are vital elements in the growth of the law but lack the
institutional consistency necessary to crystallise principles into clear-cut
obligations. Only adjudication and legislation can fulfil this function
adequately in a world of cataclysmic change. The extent to which international adjudication can play a useful part in the matter is the seventh
of the topics which I suggest as the agenda of our dispassionate dialogue.

Some of you may be aware that I have been a lifelong advocate of
extending the compulsory jurisdiction of international courts and tribunals and have written a lengthy book on the subject. From what I
have said in that book,[1] I retract nothing, here or anywhere. But the
immediate problem is not that of compulsory jurisdiction; it is that of
creating the measure of confidence without which there can be no international adjudication on either a compulsory or a voluntary basis.
Throughout the nineteenth century there was little or no compulsory
jurisdiction but an increasing volume of significant international adjudication. Today there is a wider measure of compulsory jurisdiction but the
volume and content of international adjudication is relatively less significant having regard to the volume, content and complexity of contemporary international relations. This widespread reluctance to have
recourse to international adjudication is in my judgment unhealthy for
the future of international relations and unhealthy for the future of
international law. It weakens the arrangements for the settlement of
international disputes and it deprives us of the potential contribution to
the development of the law of a substantial volume of adjudication on
significant issues. The crux of the matter is that there can be no mutual
confidence in adjudication without a common belief in the possibility of
objectivity. The creation of such a belief is not a process of intellectual
conviction; it involves an instinctive response to practical experience.
Only by putting the possibility of objectivity to the test of such experience can we create the conditions which make either objectivity or
confidence therein possible. There can be no breakthrough without risk
and courage. Can we so circumscribe the risk involved as to make it
generally acceptable?

It is understandable that conflicting ideologies and interests should be

[1] C. W. Jenks, *The Prospects of International Adjudication.* Stevens and Sons,
1964, pp. 90–118 and 757–61.

reluctant at the present early stage in the rebuilding of mutual confidence to entrust to the hazards of international adjudication acute disagreements on substantial matters in which the legal issues raised relate primarily to matters of customary law, general principles of law or equity. Nor is this reluctance confined to any one of the conflicting ideologies or interests which divide the world. In such cases the nature of the uncertainties involved maximises the difficulty of securing confidence in the objectivity of the result. What, however, of questions of fact? Many international controversies revolve around disputed facts. Fact-finding involves a much smaller element of discretionary judgment than the determination of disputed questions of law. Completely impartial procedures for the ascertainment of facts would be an immense contribution to unburdening our troubled world of fruitless controversy and tension. Should we not consider establishing and systematically using some orderly procedure for the objective determination of disputed questions of fact? Is this not a proper subject for a dispassionate dialogue?

For my part I would like to see the dialogue embrace a further possibility. When agreement has been reached upon a general convention modifying the law or creating new law we have a situation entirely different from that which exists when the law has to be deduced from custom or general principle. Whatever uncertainties may be latent in the terms of the convention are circumscribed by the measure of agreement which has been reached. In these circumstances the appropriateness of including a compulsory jurisdiction clause in general conventions should, I venture to submit, be considered quite separately from the more general question of compulsory jurisdiction in a wider range of disputes. Is it necessarily a question of principle? Can it not be considered in individual cases in the light of the circumstances of the case? Is not some measure of experiment and experience in the matter legitimate and desirable? The most favourable conditions for a significant experiment might well be reviewed in the course of our proposed dialogue. If by experiments with fact-finding procedures and the acceptance of jurisdiction in respect of disputes relating to the interpretation of carefully chosen specific conventions we could put the possibility of objectivity to the test of practical experience we should have made a major step towards rehabilitating international adjudication as a necessary element in the progress of international law.

In mature legal systems the characteristic mode of legal innovation is legislation. If we are to develop international law to meet the needs of our time a major effort of international legislation will be required. How far can we regard as adequate the techniques and resources available to us for this purpose?

During the century which has now elapsed since the conclusion of the First General Telegraphic Convention in 1865 we have made much progress by means of general conventions, which I prefer to call law-making treaties. In recent years the work of the International Law Commission of the United Nations and of the United Nations Codification Conferences, which have achieved such solid results on the basis of the work of the Commission, has been an emphatic demonstration of the part which intensive legislative effort can and should play in the consolidation and progressive development of the law. What further progress can we make in the matter? We can hardly conceive of an international legislature, comparable in composition, procedure and powers to a national legislature, being evolved within any foreseeable future. But should we not explore certain more modest possibilities?

A wide range of legislative procedures and regulatory powers for specialised purposes has been evolved by the specialised agencies of the United Nations. Among these the I.L.O. procedures for the adoption by the International Labour Conference by a two-thirds majority of conventions, which each Member then has an obligation to submit for ratification or rejection by national competent authorities, has been an outstanding success. On 1 August 1967, 110 of the 128 conventions adopted by the Conference were in force for numbers of Members varying from 2 to 99 and 3312 ratifications distributed over 122 conventions and 118 countries had been registered. The important conventions relating to fundamental human rights, which prohibit forced labour, protect freedom of association, and seek to eliminate discrimination in employment, have been particularly successful with an average of 75 and a minimum of 55 ratifications. The wider possibilities of the varied special procedures which have been evolved by the I.L.O. and other specialised agencies are worthy of sympathetic exploration.

Nor should we fail to examine how far the General Assembly can legitimately and usefully play a valuable role in fulfilling the needs of a dynamic world society for more effective legislative procedures. Certainly the General Assembly has no right to legislate in the commonly understood sense of the term, but it appears to be recognised that it may be able to exercise by general consensus functions which it has no authority under the Charter to exercise by the procedures of decision by a two-thirds or simple majority provided for in the Charter itself and that these functions may include certain functions of a legislative character. The Declaration of Legal Principles Governing the Activities of States in the Exploration and Use of Outer Space may be regarded as an authoritative formulation of spontaneous custom or a legislative act deriving its authority from general consensus. It has perhaps elements of both.[1] Viewed in the same aspect it may be an important precedent for future legislative action by the General Assembly by the same consensus procedure, which has not ceased to be such by reason of the more recent negotiation of the Treaty on Principles Governing the Activities of States in the Exploration and Use of Outer Space, including the Moon and Other Celestial Bodies. It is of interest in this connection that a recent article in *Soviet State and Law* draws a clear distinction between mandatory and recommendatory resolutions of the General Assembly and acknowledges that resolutions play an important part in the process of forming standards and if adopted without opposition may acquire binding force.[2] No dynamic society can remould its law to meet the needs of its own growth without an effective legislative procedure. Our dispassionate dialogue should therefore include the need for more effective means of international legislation and the manner in which that need can be met.

An effective rule of law in world affairs, capable of translating into reality our determination to 'live together in peace with one another as good neighbours' requires a firmer institutional framework than we have yet created. It presupposes far-reaching developments in international organisation. It implies the universality of the world community and the permanence of membership thereof, with no exclusion or expulsion from membership of any state on political grounds and no right of unilateral withdrawal from membership; the proper remedy for a gross breach of international law or morality is not to expel from membership but to compel compliance. It calls for a full recognition that the world community is a living organism, the constitutional arrangements of which must reflect the needs of the growing life of the community and be readapted as circumstances require to serve those needs. It involves the acceptance as the basis of international organisation of a recognised rule of law based on traditions of due process and respect for orderly procedure. It poses the problem of evolving modes of taking community decisions which avoid the danger that action may be paralysed—an

[1] See C. W. Jenks, *Space Law*. Stevens and Sons, 1965, pp. 183–8.
[2] M. V. Yanovsky, 'The legal force of General Assembly resolutions', *Sovyetskoye Gosudarstvo I Pravo*, No. 9, 1965, 120–4.

important element in the failure of the League of Nations—but which ensure that such decisions command general respect and have the weight necessary to make them effective in practice. It includes the question of how decisions validly taken are to be made effective in practice. These are large and complex questions; the most protracted dialogue could not do more than initiate a discussion of them, and I mention them only to avoid leaving the picture seriously incomplete.

I have attempted to outline an agenda for a dialogue. We hear much these days of coexistence as the foundation of peace. I believe in coexistence but I believe it to be possible only if it includes the coexistence of divergent ideologies governed by the rule of law. The coexistence of ideologies in the field of international law presupposes a dispassionate analysis, uninhibited by dogma, not only of principles and rules of law but of the intellectual processes by which we evolve and formulate principles of law. The dispassionate dialogue on these matters, for which I have ventured to suggest an agenda, is certainly the most fundamental and perhaps the most urgent of the tasks confronting international lawyers as they wrestle with the problem of bringing to the development of the law a creative imagination comparable to that which has transformed the political context, the economic outlook, the cultural and social climate, and the scientific and technological opportunities and dangers of our times.

2

Universality, coexistence and the rule of law[1]

We are living today through the birthpangs of a wholly new world. This traumatic experience haunts us with a dilemma to which a contemporary Greek novelist has given vivid expression:

> 'The old world is tangible, solid, we live in it and are struggling with it every moment—it exists. The world of the future is not yet born, it is elusive fluid, made of the light from which dreams are woven; it is a cloud buffeted by violent winds.'[2]

To wrestle with the unknown, like Jacob with the angel, is the greatest of all challenges to the human spirit; it is a challenge which the legal mind is predisposed, by temperament and training alike, to evade rather than to accept; it is in the nature of things that law should lag behind life. It is, therefore, not surprising that the contemporary progress of international law should still lag behind, and seriously behind, the contemporary needs of international society.

We are living in a world much newer than any of the conflicting ideologies by which we seek to interpret and remould it. All the existing political philosophies and legal theories, western and marxist, were evolved in circumstances radically different from those which now confront us. This does not in itself impair their validity, but it does call upon us to reassess their validity in the light of a human experience which now embraces wholly new perspectives. Such a continuing reassessment of fundamentals is the primary obligation of intellectual integrity in a world of revolutionary changes of cataclysmic proportions. It is a common obligation of us all which transcends all differences of ideology and allegiance. None of us can afford to live in the past.

[1] An address to the Institute of Law of the Polish Academy of Sciences, Warsaw, 13 September 1965.
[2] N. Kazantzakis, *Zorba the Greek*. Bruno Cassirier, 1959, pp. 68–9.

The relationship to each other of the three concepts of universality, coexistence and the rule of law is essentially a matter which calls for re-examination in this spirit. The subject is one which has occasioned much debate and considerable acrimony among international lawyers. The argument has re-echoed through forums as varied as the Legal Committee of the General Assembly of the United Nations, the United Nations Special Committee on the Principles of International Law Concerning Friendly Relations and Cooperation Between States, and the International Law Association. The question involves fundamentals and it is therefore not surprising that the course of the debate should have prompted deep misgivings in many quarters. Most of the existing literature, on both sides of the controversy, is dialectic rather than prophylactic; it seeks to win rather than to heal. The time has come for a fresh approach to the whole question based on a genuine attempt to find common ground.

Personally, I believe in all three of these concepts: in universality, in coexistence (which, like the General Assembly of the United Nations, I prefer to describe more positively as peaceful cooperation and friendly relations among states), and in the rule of law. I believe in them in what I believe to be their natural and plain meaning, and I believe that only in what I believe to be their natural and plain meaning are they valid, compatible with each other, or consistent with what I believe to be the nature of the human spirit.

By universality I mean that the world has become one and indivisible and needs for its health and progress a political and legal order embracing all mankind. By coexistence, or peaceful cooperation to use the more positive language preferred by the General Assembly, I mean conflicting ideologies and interests accepting the differences which divide them as recognised facts of international life and living in peace with each other as good neighbours despite those differences on the basis of tolerance, restraint and mutual respect. By the rule of law I mean an objective standard of conduct limiting the will of the state and of all states. And when I say that universality, coexistence and the rule of law are inseparable from each other, I mean that there can be no real universality without genuine coexistence, and no genuine coexistence without an effective rule of law.

I have attempted in *The Common Law of Mankind* to emphasise the obligation which our partnership in a universal world community places upon us all to develop the law of nations, the necessary foundation of the rule of law among us, as a synthesis of our varied histories and cultures rather than as an intellectual projection of any one of them claiming allegiance as of right from others. The validity of such an approach inevitably depends, as my critics among western liberals and eastern marxists alike have not been slow to insist, upon the extent to which there in fact exists at the particular time a core of common conviction and interest sufficiently significant to permit of such a synthesis. My own belief is that there is a common interest in peace, freedom and welfare which transcends ideological differences and on which patience, circumspection and magnanimity can build. But ideological differences cannot be bridged by being ignored and we can resolve our differences only by recognising them and agreeing as a conscious act to eliminate them or live with them; either choice involves important obligations and the most probable outcome is perhaps that we will choose to eliminate some of the differences and live with others.

Such an adventure can succeed only in an atmosphere of uninhibited intellectual freedom. Without freedom of speech and expression, freedom of thought is stifled; without freedom of thought there is no intellectual vitality; and without intellectual vitality we can neither seek truth and pursue it nor grapple with the practical problems of a world of cataclysmic change.

I claim no right to insist that you or anyone should share my beliefs in these matters; any such claim would be inconsistent with my own belief that I am entitled to hold my beliefs, to express them freely and fully, and to attempt to persuade others of their truth, irrespective of the extent to which you or others may share or decline to share my belief in them; claiming no monopoly of wisdom or righteousness, and no conformity from others, I recognise no obligation to conform in my own views to any dictates except those of my own conscience.

I have begun by formulating this basic intellectual approach, because it is the key to my own attitude to all these matters, and because I believe that it is also the key to any solution of the problems which we are about to discuss which can be satisfactory in the new world in which we now live.

Universality continues to be a guiding concept rather than an accepted rule of law. Our professions of the principle are profuse, but we are far from consistent in our application of it. The essence of the concept is that the world community, by reason of its nature as a universal world community, necessarily embraces within its membership and structure every political and legal order created by man on earth to govern his affairs. It is by its nature an inclusive, not an exclusive, community; and being inclusive it cannot be select or selective. It cannot, without being untrue to its own nature, and thereby partially destroying itself, reject any political or legal order as unworthy of membership. It may and should, in appropriate cases, treat certain political and legal orders as unworthy members; but the distinction is fundamental. This approach involves three consequences.

The concept of universality implies that the exclusion of the effective government of any significant state from participation in the United Nations as an instrument of policy is unjustifiable. The Charter formulates certain criteria for membership of the United Nations; the state must be peace-loving; it must accept the obligations of the Charter; and it must in the judgment of the Organisation be able and willing to carry out these obligations. These are criteria for membership, not for the recognition of the effectiveness of a change in the government of a member; even in relation to members, they do not warrant admission or exclusion on the basis of political partiality, calculation of immediate national interest, or deference to the susceptibility of public sentiment. The United Nations is not a club of pals: on the lowest estimate it is the town meeting of the world; on a more ambitious plane it is the one available nucleus for the equivalent of a common government for the world in respect of matters of common concern; on either view of its functions and future, it can play its part only if, while itself based on the clear principles enunciated in the Charter, it includes as a system of government the political systems and forces most repugnant to each other and provides a framework within which they can come to terms with each other.

The concept of universality likewise implies that the expulsion of any member from the United Nations as an instrument of policy is equally unjustifiable. The two propositions are natural corollaries of each other and cannot be disassociated. Neither aggression nor the grossest violations of human rights can be remedied by expulsion. They may justify coercive action by the community or, if it is powerless to coerce, any form of moral reprobation or suspension of particular rights or privileges of membership duly provided for by law. But expulsion is a confession of defeat by which the community, powerless to fulfil the common purpose, destroys itself.

The concept of universality also implies grave doubt whether the United Nations should readily acquiesce in the unilateral withdrawal of any member. The Charter left the legality of arbitrary withdrawal open to debate; practice has been tending towards the easy course of acquiescing in such withdrawal, apparently partly in the belief that such an attitude will facilitate the subsequent resumption of membership by avoiding an excessive hardening of irreconcilable views; whether such an attitude of restraint will be more effective for this purpose than a continued insistence that the would-be departing member remains bound by the rights and obligations of membership remains to be seen.

The Charter of the United Nations does not accept in full any of these three implications of the principle of universality. Universality as a legal concept is therefore an objective rather than a postulate of positive law; but in this as in many other respects the law lags behind life. Whether we like it or not, we are all members one of another and because we share a common destiny we constitute a universal community.

If we accept universality as one of the fundamental concepts of our approach to international law and relations, coexistence, defined as peaceful cooperation and friendly relations among states, follows as a necessary consequence.

The world dominion of a particular order may in pure logic be a possible alternative. History has known many attempts to establish a universal dominion over the known and accessible world. They have all failed. The task is now more complex than ever before. The failure of any further attempt of this nature which may be made in the future is still more certain. Both the distribution of power and the inhibitions upon its exercise preclude any such outcome. Coexistence is therefore not a philosophy to be accepted or rejected at will. It is the ineluctable destiny of man.

The concept is a fundamental one, and it is important to clarify it in positive and dynamic terms. It is the essence of coexistence that none of the partners in coexistence can dictate its terms. Any of them can destroy it. Only by mutual accommodation can they develop it.

Coexistence can have no reality as a formula for stopping short of ultimate disaster in the conduct of a ruthless struggle the parties to which continue to seek to destroy each others' way of life by all means short of the mutual extermination of the species by nuclear war. Coexistence must include the coexistence of ideologies. It must be a formula for peace, not for an uncertain armistice or the safer conduct of war. It must recognise the continued vitality of conflicting ideologies which are no longer seeking to bury each other but to live with each other. While acknowledging, respecting and upholding common international standards designed to protect the dignity and worth of the human person, it must accept the fact of continuing diversity and develop a code of conduct which enables essentially different societies to live at peace. As they live in peace with each other, some of their differences may in course of time become less significant. We cannot coexist in this manner if our minds are anchored in the past. What marxists call colonialism, and what western liberals call stalinism, are apposite illustrations of issues which now belong to the past and must be set on one side if we are to coexist in peace and freedom.

A thousand million people in fifty different countries have been granted their full political freedom in the last twenty years. Thirty-five other countries, in Europe, the Americas and the South Seas, had blazed the trail in this direction during the preceding century and a half. The process is a dynamic one and will continue. Of the colonial period there are widely varied assessments among those most directly concerned, both among the former rulers and among the former ruled. The divergences of view on the subject are much too varied, and much too complex and unpredictable in their incidence, to be explained as divergences of class outlook or economic interest. My personal view, widely though certainly not universally shared among my Asian and African friends, happens to be that, when the fullest allowance has been made for innumerable tragic mistakes and lost opportunities, some of which many of us criticised and had freedom to criticise at the time (in my own case as long as forty years ago), men will look back in centuries to come to the contribution of Britain and France during the last four centuries to human freedom and human dignity throughout the world with the same pride and gratitude with which we look back to Greece and Rome. But this we must leave to the judgment of history.

Equally clearly some of the social revolutions of the twentieth century, which have not been confined to any one part of the world or to any one political ideology, have opened up horizons of freedom previously unknown. Among these, the social revolutions of Eastern Europe will continue to represent to workers and peasants born in societies with no tradition of popular government, civil liberties, or sustained economic development, their first glimpse of broader opportunity for the common man.

Our concern now is not with the judgment of the future upon the past but with the urgent problems of the present, with securing, in the common interest of all mankind, peace, order and good government, personal and political freedom, the equality and dignity of man, economic, social and cultural advancement, the diffusion of science and technology, the rule of law, and the restraint of arbitrary power. In this great task we can and must act together, however divergent our views concerning the past may be. We can do so effectively only if we are prepared to agree that we now regard our respective errors and short-comings of the past as so completely past that we can no longer allow them to divide us. This is the principle upon which the West and the developing world are increasingly conducting their relationship; it is so solidly grounded in mutual respect and common interest that no external irritation can corrode it; and it is the only acceptable foundation for genuine coexistence on a world-wide basis.

Coexistence also implies that there will naturally exist within the universal framework of the United Nations more intimate groups of like-minded states, to some extent interlocking in membership, which are bound together by special ties of historical or geographical association; they may have a common culture, language, legal system or ideology, affinities of political, economic or social structure, or common political, economic or strategic interests. Such regional arrangements within a universal framework are not incompatible with the idea of universality. They should not be presumed to be hostile to each other in intent or effect. They may even facilitate negotiation and mutual adjustment within the universal framework. But in order to achieve such a result they must be conceived, and generally understood, to be essentially ancillary to universal action; they must be developed as an instrument of, not as an alternative to, world-wide negotiation.

How can we give institutional expression to the general policy of coexistence, so understood? The primary need is clearly a fully effective United Nations, endowed with the authority and equipped with the resources necessary to maintain the peace, control armament, secure justice, and promote economic development. But when we seek so to endow and equip the United Nations we at once encounter the dilemma, well understood by the authors of the Charter, that powerful states are reluctant to entrust their destinies to concepts and standards of objectivity which they may neither share nor respect, concepts and standards the genuine objectivity of which they may even deny. The solution envisaged by the authors of the Charter was the veto. The compromise embodied in the veto failed because the divergence of views was so wide and the depth of mistrust so great that, instead of placing a premium

c

upon negotiation to avoid the danger and odium of recourse to the veto, the veto became by repeated use a source of so much further disagreement and distrust that a sustained attempt was made for a dozen years to solve the problem by ignoring it. This attempt took the form of efforts to devise methods of action by universal organisations based on majority decision. This was, I believe, the only alternative at the time to the paralysis of the United Nations and, therefore, a necessary stage in the process of development. But in its nature it represented a departure from rather than progress towards giving institutional expression to the concept of coexistence. With changes in the composition of the United Nations it became increasingly unsatisfactory to a widening circle. We are now groping our way towards an alternative for the veto in the principle of consensus. The essence of the principle is that important matters should so far as possible be decided by agreement following full consultation and a genuine attempt to adjust conflicting views by negotiation and mutual concession. The principle is viable only if it is reasonably applied. When stated in general terms it is perhaps a counsel of wise diplomacy rather than a rule of law. Some interesting experiments are, however, now being made in giving institutional expression to it, notably in the rules of procedure of the United Nations Trade and Development Conference and in nuclear and space matters. Much may depend on how far the principle can be effectively applied to a wider range of world affairs.[1]

Giving institutional expression in this manner to the policy of coexistence is a task of greater urgency than any attempt to codify the principles of coexistence. Coexistence is not a legal principle but a historical fact which is a necessary premise for the existence and development of international law. As a recent English writer has said:

> What is important is that the *fact* of coexistence, in its broadest sense, should continue. And, for this, international law must not be emasculated, nor must international lawyers lower their standards. States with different religions, different stages of economic development and different political systems must live side by side; and a developing, flexible and strong international law must continue to provide the bridge.[2]

[1] *Cf.* C. W. Jenks, 'Unanimity, the veto, weighted voting, special and simple majorities and consensus as modes of decision in international organisations', in *Cambridge Essays in International Law: Essays in Honour of Lord McNair*, Stevens and Sons, 1965.

[2] Rosalyn Higgins, *Conflict of Interests—International Law in a Divided World*, Bodley Head 1965, p. 170.

The law can do so only if we develop adequate institutional arrangements for continuing cooperation.

As universality presupposes coexistence, so coexistence presupposes the rule of law. The principle and practice of consensus cannot bridge the gap between divergent views and conflicting interests unless there is a recognised framework of commonly accepted legal obligation within which diplomacy can operate. The rule of law is therefore fundamental to coexistence in a universal community, and implies as a minimum six things:

1. the fundamental postulate that the sovereignty of the state is the creature and not the master of the law and is therefore limited by, but does not limit, the rule of law;
2. renunciation of the right to make one's will prevail by force;
3. good faith as the basis of mutual understanding;
4. recognition that the duty of respect for legal rights and obligations on the basis of equality before the law transcends ideological preoccupations and preferences;
5. acceptance of the principle and practice of third party judgment; and
6. respect for the inherent rights of the human personality.

Without these there can be no rule of law and no coexistence in a universal community.

To meet the contemporary needs of the universal community the rule of law must also discharge two further functions: it must provide a framework for economic stability and growth throughout the world; and, it must make it possible to harness scientific and technological progress to the service of man.

Let us consider some of the implications of these essential elements in the rule of law. In the literature of coexistence the principle of 'mutual respect for the sovereignty of states' recurs constantly. If by this principle is meant respect for the right of each state to determine its own economic and social policy without external interference it presents no difficulty, but it is important that the principle should not be misconstrued.

The fundamental postulate that the sovereignty of the state is the creature and not the master of the law is the foundation of international law. It admits of no compromise; without it there can be no organised world community. Its historical origins run back to the earliest days of

all the great legal systems, as the volume *Sovereignty Within the Law*,[1]
recently sponsored by the World Rule of Law Center at Duke University, North Carolina, has so clearly shown. Different legal systems have
accepted it in different degrees at different stages of their historical
development. No legal system can claim an unblemished record in the
matter. Some measure of immunity for acts of state is conceded by
every legal system. But it is of fundamental importance whether the law
is the measure of the immunity or the immunity the measure of the law.
Unless we acknowledge that the law prevails, everything remains at the
mercy of arbitrary power. In this principle we can all find common
ground. In a recent work entitled *International Law, a Textbook for Use
in Law Schools*, the principle is stated in the following terms:

> The definitive importance of the principle of sovereignty in relations
> between states is not the same thing as the conception of 'absolute'
> sovereignty. A sovereign state must not in its international relations
> behave in an arbitrary fashion, without taking account of the generally recognised principles of international law and the international
> undertakings which it has voluntarily assumed. To do so would mean
> to violate the principle of the sovereign equality of all the members
> of the international community. It would undermine the international
> community and lead to the unlimited rule of force and violence.
>
> The question of entry into an international organisation or of the
> conclusion of a treaty is decided by each state at its own discretion.
> In such matters each state is sovereign, and no external pressure is
> permissible. But in addition to rights, entry into an international
> organisation or the conclusion of a treaty also involves certain obligations which are to a certain extent a restriction on its sovereignty.[2]

The renunciation of the right to make one's will prevail by force is
the cornerstone of the rule of law, as between individuals, as between
the state and the individual, as between states, and as between states and
international organisations. This is not a pacifist doctrine. Force plays
its part in every organised community; but within an organised community recourse to force is permitted only for the purposes sanctioned
by the law, by the procedures recognised by the law, and within the

[1] A. Larson, C. W. Jenks *et. al.*, *Sovereignty Within the Law*, Oceana, New
York, 1965.

[2] The quotation, the spirit of which completely coincides with that of the
volume sponsored by the World Rule of Law Center at Duke University, is
from the textbook issued in a number of different languages by the Institute of
Law of the Academy of Sciences of the U.S.S.R.

limits circumscribed by the law. It becomes essentially an instrument of the collective will, a safeguard for the rights and interests of both the community and its members against forcible encroachment, a last resort in emergencies subject to prompt though sometimes retrospective appraisal and approval or condemnation by legally recognised procedures. The principle is clearly set forth in the Charter of the United Nations which binds us all.

Only when the renunciation of force is followed by the renunciation of guile can we progressively create the mutual confidence in good faith without which divergent views and conflicting interests can never be reconciled. Good faith is the foundation of mutual respect. The whole of the law of treaties rests upon it. The possibility of adapting customary law to changing needs without the disintegration of the whole concept of legal obligation presupposes it. The duty to avoid unlawful harm to one's neighbour which is the basis of the international law of tort is essentially an expression of it. No progress towards a legal framework for economic stability and growth and increasing cooperation in scientific and technological matters is conceivable without it. Without the paramount obligation of good faith, the whole concept of a new world of law is a dangerous delusion. Prudent men who are conscious of their past disagreements, and of continuing divergences of ideology and interest, will naturally wish to be satisfied of each other's good faith at each successive step of their cooperation with each other. The obligation of the utmost good faith, including frankness, is no less vital to the rule of law in world affairs than the renunciation of the right to make one's will prevail by force. Aggression and subversion are the opposite sides of the same debased coin, of the bad money which drives out the good without which there can be no fruitful commerce of minds or cultures.

Neither the renunciation of force, of violence, nor the renunciation of guile, of fraud and deceit, can be effective if it is subject in our minds or practice to an implied ideological qualification. The duty of respect for legal rights and obligations on the basis of equality before the law transcends ideological preoccupations and preferences. The renunciation of force and the obligation of good faith protect us because they apply objectively to all. We can claim and enjoy their protection only by respecting them objectively.

Here we touch upon a fundamental point. Our estimate of the part which the rule of law can play in world affairs will depend on the extent to which we recognise the possibility of objectivity. The vital question is not the extent to which we are satisfied that particular institutions at particular times afford sufficient guarantees of objectivity, but the measure in which we accept the basic concept that objectivity is something possible and desirable. There can be no rule of law in a society in which everyone remains the judge of his own rights. The concept of third party judgment implies the acceptance of the possibility of objectivity. The primary difficulty is the fluidity in world affairs which we have accepted as the point of departure of the discussion. In a static society, objectivity can be measured by standards which are generally accepted as objective. The rules are known, and the margin of judgment involved in their application is limited. In a dynamic society, objectivity consists of an attitude of fairness rather than a fixed angle of approach; there is no objective standard of objectivity. Uncertainty in the law is implied in the nature of the society. We must therefore choose between the risk that the law will prove uncongenial and the risk that, if we reject the uncertain arbitrament of the law, the facts may prove still more uncongenial. The essence of the rule of law is willingness to recognise the possibility of fairness in the determination of disputed matters and to abide by the result. The result will not always be palatable, but the method and its results, taken as a whole, are more palatable than the only possible alternative, namely the principle of every man for himself and the devil take the hindmost.

My own conclusion from this approach is that we should accept in a changing world the risks of compulsory jurisdiction on the broadest possible basis and seek the creative development of the law by international courts and tribunals by an imaginative recourse to general legal principle, equity and considerations of international public policy. I believe that all of us have less to lose by such boldness than by any other possible course of action. My views on the matter are set forth in full in *The Prospects of International Adjudication* and I neither recant nor qualify them here nor anywhere. But as a pragmatist with thirty-five years' experience of practical international life, I recognise that all this may take a little time, especially on a world-wide basis. Is there any more immediate step which can profitably be envisaged? Is there an area within which respect for objectivity can be achieved now?

Does not the determination of disputed facts constitute such an area? Questions of fact loom large in many international controversies. Nothing is more corrosive of good faith and mutual confidence than stubborn disagreement concerning alleged facts which one party believes or assumes to have been fully established and the other party knows or believes to be false or misunderstood. If we can take disputed facts out of the range of subjective appreciation, we may have taken an important step towards establishing the possibility of objectivity in a divided world. The idea is, of course, not new; it was one of the commonplaces of the Hague Conferences of 1899 and 1907. The General Assembly, by a majority vote, recently requested the Secretary-General to make a study of the matter, but the proposal has thus far failed to evoke any general enthusiasm. One may, however, reasonably hope that the general idea may prove to have a new application of major importance at the present juncture of world affairs, and may in course of time command increasing support.

Can we perhaps conceive that some agreed initiative in the matter might be taken in the relatively near future in the General Assembly of the United Nations? Might not the General Assembly place it on record that any state aggrieved by a factual allegation concerning it should be entitled as a matter of right to have the facts established by an impartial body whose findings would be made known to the whole world? Could not some appropriate authority, perhaps the Secretary-General of the United Nations, be empowered to make arrangements for establishing the facts at the request of the aggrieved party without delay? Would it not be wise for the Security Council and the General Assembly to make a practice of suspending judgment on disputed questions of fact, as distinguished from any measures necessary to deal with an immediate threat to a breach of the peace, pending the outcome of such an inquiry? If such an approach commands general support, why cannot action be taken in the matter at an early date? If there are valid objections to such an approach, why cannot they be reasonably stated and accompanied by some constructive alternative proposal as a basis for further discussion?

Once we have established an agreed method for treating questions of fact as questions of fact and questions of evidence as questions of evidence we may have taken the decisive first step towards treating questions of law as questions of law, even in a dynamic and divided world. We will have re-established belief in the possibility of objectivity, the objectivity which President Winiarski, as President of the International Court of Justice, so conspicuously exemplified. We can then proceed together to the following stage of considering the range within which objectivity is acceptable and the extent of our common willingness to abide by its unpredictable results. In so doing we must never overlook the element of reciprocity in these matters. The compulsory jurisdiction, or bold exercise of judicial authority, which we find so irritating today may be vital for the protection of our own rights and interests tomorrow.

The process may take some time, but meanwhile we can be well content to walk awhile in company before we try to run in harness with each other.

The relationship between the rule of law among states and the rule of law within states has been much debated; in logic there may be no necessary connection between the two, but they presuppose the same habits of mind and for this reason there is a political and psychological connection between them repeatedly attested by the witness of history. Respect by the state for the inherent rights of the human personality therefore takes its place among the essential elements of the rule of law. There could be no more dramatic contribution to human reconciliation dedicated to the freedom and dignity of man than more effective common action for the international protection of human rights.

The unanimous adoption by the General Assembly of the United Nations Covenants of Human Rights opens up new perspectives of progress, but much remains to be done to make the Covenants a reality. For the time being they are a magnificent opportunity rather than a solid achievement. Their practical value will depend in large measure on three conditions which still remain to be fulfilled. They must be widely and promptly ratified; they must be ratified without reservations which detract significantly from the obligations which they embody; the procedures of implementation for which they provide must be applied with the highest standards of thoroughness and objectivity. Only when these conditions are fulfilled will the Covenants become the living law of the United Nations family.

Without prejudice to the long-term effect and effectiveness of the Covenants, or the continued validity of such important regional guarantees of human rights as the European Convention for the Protection of Human Rights and Fundamental Freedoms and the analogous arrangements being discussed in the Americas and in Africa, we could usefully supplement them by measures to increase their practical effectiveness in certain crucial areas. Could we not envisage the negotiation of a series of simple conventions formulating, with a minimum of procedural or other detail, some of the basic civil liberties enunciated by the Universal Declaration of Human Rights in the form of obligations accepted as such by states? I venture to suggest an experiment along these lines consisting in the first instance of three simple conventions, each to be concluded as a separate instrument so that any state prevented by some unanticipated difficulty from becoming a party to one would not be debarred from ratifying the others. The first would establish the presumption of innocence until proof of guilt. The second would preclude guilt by association. The third would prohibit retroactive penalties. I believe that such a group of conventions could be of considerable practical value in securing more effective application of the United Nations Covenant on Civil and Political Rights. In the light of the experience acquired with them consideration could be given subsequently to the possibility of further progress in respect of more difficult matters. There might, for instance, be a second stage consisting of a group of conventions relating to freedom from arbitrary arrest or detention, provision for prompt trial, and freedom of religious observance, and at each successive stage the progress made and possibility of further progress could be reviewed. In this manner we could progressively make international action for the protection of human rights on a world-wide basis increasingly effective.

Civil liberties are not in themselves a guarantee of economic wellbeing and, though man does not live by bread alone, he has not learned to live without bread or, failing bread, rice. In every type of society and economy the law is increasingly concerned with the problems of economic stability and growth, with welfare as freedom's twin. This preoccupation is inevitably reflected in the contemporary development of international law. It calls for a generous and sustained collective effort, in which we must all take part, to promote by trade and aid, in a disinterested manner and where possible by combined action within the common framework of the United Nations, 'better standards of life in larger freedom' everywhere. One important test of our contribution to such a collective effort is our willingness to accept the mutual obligations, and contribute the financial and other resources, necessary for this purpose.

The field for collective action is rapidly extending beyond the traditional scope for trade and aid to new fields of science and technology. To provide a legal framework within which the resources of advanced science and technology can be mobilised for the benefit of all mankind is perhaps the greatest of the tasks confronting international lawyers in our time. We are making some tentative progress in the matter notably in respect of nuclear energy and space. The Declaration of Legal Principles Governing the Activities of States in the Exploration and Use of Outer Space and the Treaty on Principles Governing the Activities of States in the Exploration and Use of Outer Space, including the Moon and Other Celestial Bodies, are important landmarks in the formulation by agreement of a body of common principles on the basis of which we can proceed together to deal stage by stage with the innumerable practical problems which will arise. The part played in what has been achieved thus far by Professor Manfred Lachs as Chairman of the Legal Sub-Committee of the United Nations Committee on the Peaceful Uses of Outer Space deserves special tribute.

I make no claim to have solved these various problems which I have adumbrated. By their nature they cannot be solved by any cut and dried formula. What I have attempted to do is to define a frame of mind in which we can seek together to grope our way towards their solution, conscious that in true knowledge there is little certainty but much awareness of the perpetual challenge of the infinite. We should approach the matter in the spirit of Professor Grigori Tunkin's plea that we should free legal science 'from dogmatism, from the use of citations instead of creative legal thought' and recognise that our aim 'must not only be knowledge of what exists in international law but active participation in changing it'.[1] In dogma the elusiveness of truth is frozen into immobility; the future of the world community, the future of human society, the future of human life, belong not to any rival ideology, yours or mine, but to the freedom of the human spirit. Let us all say with Adam Mickiewicz:

> I shall beat one wing against the past,
> The other against the future,
> And steering by the dictates of the heart,
> Strive towards the feet of God.

I trust that you will allow me to transpose the words of your own historic anthem. The world community of peace and freedom

> is not lost forever
> While our lives remain.

[1] As quoted in E. McWhinney, *Peaceful Coexistence and Soviet-Western International Law*, A. W. Sythoff, Leiden, 1964, p. 16.

3

Sovereignty today[1]

There is no more important issue in contemporary international law than the future of sovereignty. While the concept of the state as the creature and instrument rather than the master of the law is common to a wide range of western and non-western legal systems[2], the modern world owes it primarily to the western tradition; in the western tradition the concept derives from Greek political thought as transmitted to modern times through Roman law and medieval scholasticism. In ancient Greece we can trace the concept back to Homeric times; it was the essence of the conception of the *polis*; but it was in Athens that the conception came to fruition as the point of departure of western political thought. Plato deviated from it in *The Republic* only to revert to it in *The Laws*; Aristotle was its consistent champion. The concept of 'a government of laws and not of men' goes back to ancient Greece.

Athens offers warning as well as inspiration to the student of sovereignty. There is a marked analogy between the breakdown of the Greek polity following the Peloponnesian War and the political crisis of western civilisation in our own time. In both cases the essence of the problem was that the sovereignty of the traditional political units had outlived its usefulness. In ancient times the Macedonian and Roman empires served as successive vehicles through which Greek culture continued to fertilise the world. Today we are groping towards a world order which can fulfil the same function. In the years from 1914 to 1945 the western world destroyed its political supremacy in its Peloponnesian War; the future of its political and legal traditions and its culture will depend on the success of this process of groping beyond sovereignty.

Paradoxically, the recrudescence of sovereignty is one of the leading hallmarks and headaches of our time. Thirty years ago apologists for sovereignty were *rara aves* among international lawyers. The First

[1] An address to the Panteios School of Political Science, Athens, 17 December 1964.
[2] See Larson, Jenks *et al.*, *Sovereignty Within the Law*, 1965.

World War had shattered the belief in the sovereign state. The intellectual henchmen of Hegel had been subdued by arms, and by weapons still more powerful than arms: ideas. Those of Marx and Sorel had not yet made their bid to dominate the world. Something of the optimism of the period preceding the First World War reappeared as a kind of afterglow in the days of 'the spirit of Locarno'. We all agreed with Sir Frederick Pollock that 'the doctrine of sovereignty has been found inadequate, like all dogmatic formulas, to account for complex facts'.[1] It was widely assumed that the erosion of sovereignty had become an inevitable, and would prove to be an accelerating, process.

Today the position is still more complex. The erosion of sovereignty continues, but claims to sovereignty are more widely and perhaps more vigorously asserted than ever before. This is the almost inevitable result of the doubling in less than twenty years of the number of independent states in the world and the aspiration of the new states to full and obvious control of their affairs. The natural claim of new states to enjoy in full all that their predecessors claimed in their prime poses a major problem. Sovereignty is, moreover, a bulwark behind which groups in the international community which find themselves in a minority are apt to retrench themselves, and this appears to have been an important element in the continued emphasis placed upon sovereignty by international lawyers from communist states.

How far does the concept of sovereignty epitomise the ideals and aspirations of the new states in a manner which gives it a new title to our respect? How far is it important in the continuing debate concerning coexistence in a divided world? How far is it, as we of my generation assumed in our youth, a snare and a delusion? The cult of sovereignty is characteristic of the tendency of political and legal thought to be parasitic upon things as they have been rather than perceptive of things as they are or purposeful concerning things as they might be.

There is, of course, a copious literature concerning the matter,[2] but much of it relates to sovereignty as a historical concept or intellectual abstraction rather than to the contemporary political problem. Sovereignty as traditionally understood is, in origin and essence, the conceptual expression of a dominant political fact. It is not in itself a fact but a theory or assumption concerning the facts of authority and power, the

[1] Sir Frederick Pollock (F. Pollock), *An Introduction to the History of the Science of Politics*, Mayflower Books, 1960, p. 98.
[2] See, e.g. F. H. Hinsley, *Sovereignty*, C. A. Watts and Co., 1966, and literature there cited at pp. 237–41.

legal facet of a claim that unrestrained power which brooks no discipline by law or higher authority is the basis of the effectiveness of the state and the peace and security of its citizens. So regarded it has a double aspect, that of supreme political power within the state and that of the absence of any comparable power over the state. The staunchest protagonists of the concept are constrained to admit that, over the long and wide sweep of history, the sovereignty of the state has been the exception rather than the rule even within the state.[1] Hobbes himself acknowledged 'how different this Doctrine is from the practice of the greatest part of the world' and the experience of subsequent centuries has confirmed the accuracy of Leibniz's prognosis that all human authority is necessarily relative and conditional. They nevertheless regard the evolution of the concept as proof of the maturity of the state. As applied to international relations the concept in its traditional form implies that the parts have a final and absolute authority denied to the whole. No subsequent insistence that this gives us a realistic framework for the development of international relations on the basis of a fuller recognition by states of their mutual responsibilities to each other can transform this final and absolute authority of the parts into an effective mutual discipline on behalf of the whole.

Sovereignty can, of course, be reconstructed as a residuum of discretionary authority circumscribed by law, but if it is envisaged in this manner the emotional undertones of the concept may make it both wiser and easier to reject it than to refine it.

Can we in these circumstances reasonably accept the doctrine of sovereignty as the culmination of, or must we not rather regard it as an aberration in, the development of political institutions and the progress of political and legal analysis and philosophy? Is there not a considerable arrogance, compounded by remoteness from the urgencies of the nuclear age and insufficient practical experience of the variety, complexity and mutability of the internal structure and mutual relations of states, in the assumption of some theoretical writers on sovereignty that they alone have understood the nature and true character of the problems involved and that those who regard the concept as immoral or outmoded have failed to understand its function or to come to grips with reality?

For my part I still believe the concept of sovereignty as traditionally and commonly understood to be a snare and a delusion, which the new states will quickly recognise as such as they find that it cannot fulfil any of the essential purposes for which they value their freedom and

[1] *Cf.* Larson, Jenks *et al.*, *Sovereignty Within the Law*, 1965.

independence and which cannot serve effectively the long-term interest of either party to the ideological conflict. It is not a healthy consecration by law of a reality of power necessary to the effectiveness of the state, but an illusion which converts the reality of power, which, however real, is never absolute, into a miasma of irresponsibility. The essence of the matter is of the utmost simplicity. The world has outgrown sovereignty. Sovereignty is not the glory of manhood, which the young covet as they see the old relinquish it in impotence, but, if I may be forgiven for mis-appropriating Lenin's phrase, 'an infantile disorder'. Sovereignty holds no promise of peace; it affords no prospect of defence; it provides no assurance of justice; it gives no guarantee of freedom; it offers no hope of prosperity; it furnishes no prescription for welfare; it disrupts the discipline without which scientific and technological change becomes the Frankenstein of our society. It is a mockery, not a fulfilment, of the deepest aspirations of humanity. As was said by George Scelle in his last article,[1] 'if external sovereignty, so-called, is to remain the apanage of a hundred states, each determining for itself the content of its discretionary powers, we would do well to say with the poet "abandon hope"; we will remain for ever at the gates of hell.'

Let me, returning from Dante to contemporary international politics and the methodology of the common law, elaborate somewhat this bill of particulars of my indictment. The indictment has been drawn against the mysticism of sovereignty. It does not lie against the rational reinterpretation of sovereignty as the rights recognised by the law to be inherent in the status of full membership in the organised international community.[2] But it is red-blooded sovereignty as invoked by the spokesmen of governments impatient of restraint, and by scholars whose frustration with the study and the classroom find expression in a cynicism miscalled realism, not the reinterpretation of the concept by the more sophisticated, in the worlds of thought and action alike, which constitutes the immediate practical problem by reason of which the indictment is necessary. And the judgment which the indictment seeks is no less political than moral and juristic. Red-blooded sovereignty is a moral enormity and a juristic monstrosity, but the decisive count against it is that it cannot, by its very nature, fulfil the true end of man in political

[1] Prof. Ténékides, *ed.*, *Mélanges Séfériadès*, 1961, Vol. I, pp. 3–12: 'si . . . la soi-disant souveraineté extérieure doive rester l'apanage de cent Etats, déclarant eux-mêmes le contenu de leurs compétences discrétionnaires, mieux vaut dire avec le poète: "Lasciate ogni esperanza": nous resterons toujours aux portes de l'enfer.'

[2] *Cf.* Larson, Jenks *et al.*, *Sovereignty within the Law*, 1965, pp. 14–15.

society. The most eloquent refutation of sovereignty is its futility. Let us test this proposition by the professed purposes of contemporary politics.

Sovereignty and peace

Peace is the supreme need of international society. Without peace there can be neither justice, nor freedom, nor prosperity, nor welfare. Sovereignty, as traditionally understood, holds no promise of peace. Its most extreme expression was indeed the right of war, now renounced by treaty. It is still invoked to dispute the principle of third-party judgment. It still seeks to circumscribe, in the interest of the continuing freedom of action of each state, the weighing and adjustment of conflicting interests, by negotiation or decision, without which the causes and occasions of armed conflict cannot be eliminated. It remains resistant to vesting in international bodies the powers of decision, regulation and management necessary for the effective protection of the interests of the world community as a whole in such vital areas as arms control, nuclear energy and space. There can be no peace without the renunciation of war, the acceptance of third-party judgment, the resolute adjustment of conflicts of interest before they generate strains and tensions which defy social control, the common regulation and common management of common interests on behalf of the world community as a whole. Sovereignty, as traditionally understood, offers us none of these; all of them presuppose the rule of law buttressed by effective institutional arrangements.

Sovereignty and defence

When peace is precarious, defence may be one of the main safeguards of peace itself; when peace fails us, defence becomes paramount. Sovereignty, as traditionally understood, affords no prospect of defence. It was an ineffective protection even when it was still possible for all major and many lesser states to maintain armed forces of significant military importance. The part played by alliances in political and military history throughout the ages, and the constant preoccupation of statesmen and strategists with the balance of power, are a sufficient demonstration of the extent to which effective defence has long presupposed collective action transcending the concept of sovereignty. Even the strongest states no longer rely for their defence exclusively upon their sovereignty and the control which it gives them of their national military forces. The U.S.A. is a partner in NATO, CENTO, SEATO, and the ANZUS and Rio Treaties; the U.S.S.R. is a partner in the Warsaw Treaty; China has analogous arrangements with her neighbours. The defence of Western Europe still rests essentially upon NATO, despite recent changes. The Organisation of American States and the Organisation of African Unity both represent continental approaches, no less significant because they fall far short of being fully effective, to the problem of defence and security. For nations great and small a rational defence policy must now rest upon obligations and habits of mutual restraint, measures of collective support, arms control arrangements designed to maintain a reasonable equilibrium, and safeguards based upon mutual verification. We have not yet made a reality of these mutually complementary elements in any rational policy, but they are generally recognised primary objectives of current statesmanship.

Sovereignty and justice

Neither peace nor security can be divorced from justice and in the Charter of the United Nations the three concepts are rightly presented as a trinity; without justice, peace will not endure and security will prove illusory.

Justice presupposes two things: that recourse to law is available to all and that the law itself is just and responsive to changing needs. Sovereignty, as traditionally understood, provides no assurance of justice in either respect. It continues to be pleaded as an objection to extending the compulsory jurisdiction on international courts and tribunals; but without compulsory jurisdiction access to legal process is precarious, and justice delayed is no less justice denied in the world of the United Nations than in the world of Magna Carta. The whole concept is, moreover, a major barrier to the growth of the law in response to changing needs. Only by a statesmanlike recourse to general legal principle, equity and public policy can the law, which by its nature is the creature of the past, respond creatively to the needs of the future. Such a dialogue between past and future is the essence of legal development in every living legal system. Sovereignty, as traditionally understood, makes access to legal process precarious and inhibits the creative development of the law. Only the rule of law buttressed by effective institutional arrangements offers any assurance that recourse to law is available to all and that the law itself is just and responsive to changing needs.

Sovereignty and freedom

Peace and justice are among the good things of life; without them the life of society is 'nasty, brutish and short'; but peace is not an end in itself and justice is as much a means as an end. Both are avenues to freedom. Indeed the passion for freedom furnishes much of the emotional content of the claims made for sovereignty. The ultimate test of political freedom is the manner in which it is reflected in personal freedom. The freedom of the State has no inherent virtue; the objective is the freedom of man. Sovereignty, as traditionally understood, gives no guarantee of freedom to either the state or the citizen. It does not protect the freedom of the state. The freedom from restraint which it proclaims either leaves every state exposed to the arbitrary conduct of rival sovereignties or is so limited by the duty to respect rival sovereignties that it ceases to be freedom from restraint. In practice the emotional connotation of the term tends to play down the element of respect for rival sovereignties and to emphasise the element of freedom from restraint with all that that implies in unbridled anarchy. The renunciation of armed force may afford protection against the cruder forms of violence applied across frontiers by armed force; it affords no effective protection against subversion or economic aggression; it leaves vested rights and vital interests at the mercy of arbitrary irresponsibility.

Still less does sovereignty protect the freedom of man. It leaves the rights and freedoms proclaimed by the Universal Declaration of Human Rights and the United Nations Covenants of Human Rights utterly at the mercy of arbitrary power. Freedom of thought, freedom of speech, freedom of association; freedom from arbitrary arrest, detention or exile; due process and fair trial; freedom from retroactive punishment and guilt by association; these are the basic civil liberties on which human freedom rests. Sovereignty, as traditionally understood, furnishes no guarantee of any of these things; they can be so secured only by so expanding the rule of law, buttressed by appropriate institutional arrangements, that the effective protection of the rights of man is recognised as a major responsibility of international society.

Sovereignty and prosperity

Neither peace nor freedom rests upon a solid basis without prosperity. Freedom from want is no less vital than freedom from fear to the stability and progress of international society. Sovereignty, as traditionally understood, offers no hope of prosperity. The freedom of action in respect of currency, trade, migration and suchlike matters which were one of its most characteristic expressions, and even regarded a generation ago as of its essence, gave us the great depression and economic anarchy

D

which preceded and produced the Second World War. These are things of the past. We still hear much of economic sovereignty, and such expressions as 'permanent sovereignty over natural resources' have become widely current, but currency and tariffs, investment and trade, have increasingly become matters for collective discussion and decision. The trend first emerged clearly in the measure of cooperation under-taken by the more developed countries to promote greater economic stability, measures typified by the International Monetary Fund, the General Agreement on Tariffs and Trade and the Organisation for Economic Cooperation and Development. The emphasis of such cooper-ation has gradually shifted from economic stability to economic growth. The United Nations Conference on Trade and Development has made it certain that this trend will continue and increasingly shape the policies of countries in all stages of development. Fair prices for primary pro-ducts; the availability of import requirements; compensatory financing to mitigate short-term fluctuations in export earnings; long-term supple-mentary financing when necessary to offset a long-term decline of export earnings; greater use of the world's money markets for financing development; trade preferences for the manufactured products of developing countries; these are the recognised objectives of the 'seventy-five'. Sovereignty, as traditionally understood, offers no hope of any of these things; they can be secured only by so expanding the rule of law, buttressed by appropriate institutional arrangements, that it becomes the accepted basis of international economic life.

Sovereignty and welfare

Affluence alone will not suffice to eliminate the economic causes of war. The test of prosperity is its contribution to welfare. There can, in the language of the Preamble to the Constitution of the International Labour Organisation, 'be no lasting peace without social justice'. Sovereignty, as traditionally understood, furnishes no prescription for welfare. It may mask an arrogant refusal by privilege to subordinate the selfishness of the few to the needs of the many. Such refusal may perpet-uate and embitter both the East-West and the North-South conflicts. It may aggravate social tensions which threaten the structure of society everywhere. It may create an invincible reluctance in the advanced countries to maintain and expand necessary policies of development aid. It is an illusion to suppose that the rich countries will continue to tax their poor to fill the pockets of the rich in the poor countries; riches and poverty are relative expressions and resources gladly made available for the common welfare will not be made available for any considerable period of time to store up corrupt social systems. Equality of educational opportunity, full employment, equitable tax systems, agrarian reform, social security, sound industrial relations: these are among the essential elements of a healthy society in the contemporary world. Sovereignty, as traditionally understood, promises none of these things; they can be secured only by so expanding the rule of law, buttressed by appropriate institutional arrangements, that it becomes the accepted basis of the promotion of the common welfare, within as well as among states.

Sovereignty and science

We are seeking a peace of justice and freedom, prosperity and welfare, in a world which is being remoulded each passing hour by the impact of science and technology. Sovereignty is no match for Frankenstein. Human ingenuity has released forces which no sovereignty, as traditionally understood, can hope to control. Protection against nuclear dangers, against space contamination and the more immediate threat of large-scale pollution of the atmosphere, ground waters and the seas, and against environmental changes which may disrupt the whole ecological balance of human life: these things no sovereignty, as traditionally understood, can hope to give us; they can be secured only by so expanding the rule of law, buttressed by appropriate institutional arrangements, that science and technology remain man's servant and do not become his master.

The validity of these considerations is increasingly widely recognised. They have been aptly summarised in a recent study of the changing temper of British foreign policy:

> Sovereignty in the practical sense loses much of its value if it does not in practice give a nation control of its own affairs, and the fact is that neither Britain nor any of the larger powers of Europe can now have the kind of national control of their own affairs which they enjoyed in the past. In major military and economic policies they have only the choice between two alternative forms of dependence. They can either maintain formal sovereignty, while remaining none the less dependent, as smaller nations have always been, on the decisions of larger powers; or they can join together in pooling their sovereignty with others so as to form a bigger political unit, strong enough to be a great power in modern conditions and to enjoy something like the freedom

of action which was available to them as separate nation states in the past.[1]

These considerations are applicable in full to all but the largest, and applicable in large measure to even the largest, of the states of the modern world.

The bill of particulars is now complete. A grand jury consisting largely of newly-independent states must now decide whether to uphold the indictment. Their decision will affect profoundly, and may indeed determine, both the future of the world and their own future, indeed the future of the human race. The decision may well be delayed, but I do not believe that the bill of indictment which I have drawn will be lightly rejected. Too much is at stake, and there are too many indications of a wide appreciation of how much is at stake. Two immensely significant facts qualify the insistence of new states upon their sovereignty. The routine of independence for a new state has come to consist of two parts: the hoisting of its flag in the national capital when the new government takes office and, within a few days thereafter, the hoisting of its flag at the United Nations when the new state proudly assumes membership of the organised international community. Dag Hammarskjöld, speaking with prescience on 7 March 1956, before the African states were added to those of Asia in the growing membership of the United Nations, said:

> It is natural for old and well-established countries to see in the United Nations a limitation on their sovereignty. It is just as natural that a young country, a country emerging on the world stage, should find in the United Nations an addition to its sovereignty, an added means of speaking to the world.[2]

The interdependence symbolised by membership of the United Nations has thus become the recognised corollary of independence, the accepted wider framework within which independence seeks fulfilment. Equally significant is the tendency of new and indeed of all developing states to muster their collective strength to speak to the world with a united voice. The Organisation of American States, the Organisation of African Unity, and the emergence at the United Nations Conference on Trade and Development in 1964 of the group of seventy-five developing countries cannot be disregarded in any estimate of the extent to which sovereignty represents the reality of politics or the decisive ideology of

[1] K. Younger, *Changing Perspectives in British Foreign Policy*, Oxford U.P. for R.I.I.A., 1964, p. 91.
[2] Dag Hammarskjöld, *Servant of Peace*, Bodley Head, 1962, p. 134.

the contemporary world; they are the natural counterpart of NATO, the Council of Europe and the Organisation for Economic Cooperation and Development among the developed countries of the West or, in the Communist world, of the Council of Mutual Economic Assistance; they underline the extent to which the concept of sovereignty is an intellectual and emotional hangover. Tentative gropings as these developments may sometimes prove to be in practice, and uncertain as their future may still be, they reaffirm decisively the principle evolved in ancient Greece that sovereignty is not enough. They demonstrate clearly that the doctrine of sovereignty is as alien to the needs and interests of the modern world as the theory of the divine right of kings.

Why, in these circumstances, need we concern ourselves further with the matter? Cannot we now be content to forget the part which sovereignty, as traditionally understood, has played in the traditional thinking of political philosophers and international lawyers? We have, alas, not yet sufficiently purged ourselves of the past for this to be either wise or possible. The old Adam is still all too apt to plunge us back into the original sin of a self-sufficient approach to problems which call for a wider outlook. Mr Justice Holmes once said that 'theory is the most important part of the dogma of the law, as the architect is the most important man who takes part in the building of a house'.[1] While the dogma of sovereignty retains its grip, the creative approach required to build a house of many mansions for human freedom and human dignity will continue to be inhibited. Let us therefore discard the dogma of sovereignty, reaffirm with so many of our forefathers that the only sovereignty we acknowledge is that of the law, and so release our creative faculties that we can, by expanding the rule of law buttressed by appropriate institutional arrangements, build together the prosperity and welfare of a free commonwealth, in which peace and justice rest solidly upon the common law of mankind.

[1] O. W. Holmes, *Collected Legal Papers*, Constable, 1921, p. 200.

4

The new dimensions of international law[1]

In the western world we learn as children from the Book of Daniel of 'the law of the Medes and the Persians, which altereth not'.[2] We are all too apt to forget that Darius the King, after committing Daniel to the den of lions in deference to this avowed principle, renounced it, amending his own decree that petitions should be made exclusively to himself, by providing that all men should honour the God who had delivered Daniel from the power of the lions.[3] The moral of the story is not that good law altereth not, but that a law which altereth not may fail to do justice. There is also implicit in the story a second moral: that justice and the exclusive authority of the state may be incompatible with each other. There is therefore no historical paradox in my having chosen to address you, the Medes and the Persians of our time, on the changeability of law in the world society of today in which the state can no longer claim the exclusive allegiance of honourable men. I do so, moreover, with the less hesitation as 'the revision of the laws and their conformity with the needs of the time' was one of the major objectives of policy enunciated by His Majesty Mohamed Reza Shah Pahlavi in his first address to Parliament on 16 September 1941.

There is in your heritage an abiding inspiration which belies the dogma of law 'which altereth not'. The concepts of the continuous choice between good and evil, of thought which fills the world with light, of the golden age as a vocation to be pursued, not a nostalgic legend to be mourned, and of the cosmic scale as the measure of man's destiny, all go back to Zoroaster.

There are, moreover, a number of other elements in Iranian tradition which are of immense significance for the legal order of contemporary world society. It has been well said that among the achievements of the

[1] An address at the Faculty of Law of the University of Teheran, 11 December 1966.
[2] Daniel 6:8.   [3] Daniel 6:26–7.

Achaemenids 'the concept of "one world", the fusion of peoples and cultures in one "oecumene", was one of the important legacies to Alexander and the Romans'.[1] The empires of Assyria and Egypt, of India and China, and the decentralised polity of Greece, were all expressions of single and related cultures. The Achaemenid Empire was the first political bridge between East and West, the link between Plato and Asoka. The Achaemenid tradition was one of multi-cultural tolerance. We all recall that it was Cyrus who freed the Jews from the Babylonian captivity. It was under Persian rule that the Torah became the law of Israel and the ancient laws of Egypt were codified.

A thousand years later Iran again played an oecumenical role in the transformation of Islam from a heritage of the Arabian desert into a multi-national and multi-lingual culture and faith widely spread over three continents. Iranian civilisation played in the development of Islam a part analogous in this respect to that which Hellenic civilisation had played in the development of Christianity.

In the light of this long tradition of tolerance of diversity it is not surprising that the first codification of the rules of international law governing the coexistence of two distinct cultures of which we have record should be in the treaties concluded in A.D. 561–2 between Justinian and Chosroes[2]—treaties dealing with matters such as embassies, treaty practice, the treatment of aliens, and the protection of minorities, which have all continued to preoccupy the International Law Commission of the United Nations in our own day.

These are not matters belonging to the past which have no continuing significance for the present and the future. They are living traditions which remain directly relevant to the immediate problems confronting the world community in the Middle Eastern region as in the world at large. These problems arise from the precarious balance of nuclear terror, the still growing gap between affluence and stunted economic development, the persistent tendency of scientific and technological innovation to outrun social control, and the blunting of morality and humanity in a world which has hardened itself to horror. These are the fundamental problems of our society and how far international law is of any real importance for the future of mankind depends on its relevance to their solution.

[1] R. N. Frye, *The Heritage of Persia*, Weidenfeld & Nicolson, 1962, p. 125.
[2] S. Verosta, 'International Law in Europe and Western Asia between 100 and 650 A.D.', *Recueil des Cours de l'Académie de Droit International*, vol. 3, 1964, pp. 491–613, especially at pp. 597–611.

The complexity and urgency of these problems poses four acute issues concerning the place of law in the contemporary world community. These are:

1. the relationship of law to force in maintaining the peace, order and good government of the community;
2. the relationship of law to the economic stability and growth of the community;
3. the relationship of law to the social control of scientific and technological development on behalf of the community;
4. the relationship of law to the moral sense and human values of the community.

None of these issues can be resolved to the satisfaction of the modern mind and conscience by the concept of a law 'which altereth not'. Each presupposes a vigorous creative development of the law as we inherited it.

It is for this reason that some of the broader questions posed by the equal division of opinion in the International Court of Justice in the *South West Africa Case* are of such far-reaching importance for the future of international law. Seven members of the Court (who became a majority by the casting vote of the President) said in the judgment that the duty of the Court 'is to apply the law as it finds it, not to make it'.[1] An equal number of judges did not regard this proposition as justifying the dismissal of the claim brought by Ethiopia and Liberia that South Africa had violated the terms of the mandate by the practice of *apartheid*. One of the dissentient judges, Kotaro Tanaka, a legal philosopher and historian of exceptional repute, who had served previously as Chief Justice of Japan, described the historical development of law as demonstrating 'the continual process of the cultural enrichment of the legal order by taking into consideration values or interests which had previously been excluded from the sphere of law'.[2] Conceding that a court of law does not legislate, he continued,

> Where the borderline can be drawn is a very delicate and difficult matter. Of course, judges declare the law, but they do not function automatically. We cannot deny the possibility of some degree of creative element in their judicial activities. What is not permitted to judges is to establish the law independently of an existing legal system, institution or norm. What is permitted to them is to declare

[1] 1966 I.C.J. 48.   [2] *Ibid.*, 252.

what can be logically inferred from the *raison d'être* of a legal system, institution or norm. In the latter case the lacuna in the intent of legislation or parties can be filled.[1]

The issue thus so clearly joined has applications far wider than the immediate question of South West Africa and may well be with us for a generation. Let us test it by a brief discussion of three questions of far-reaching contemporary importance, the legal consequences of the creation of corporate personality for international purposes, international liability for ultra-hazardous activities, and (stating in general terms the question which came before the Court in the *South West Africa Case* in a specific and highly special context) the extent to which a legitimate concern for the common welfare constitutes a legal interest entitling a state to seek the performance of an international obligation in the discharge of which it has no individualised material interest. Each of these questions illuminates the critical nature of the present phase of development in a major unsettled area of the law. Each of them is related to some of the most significant developments of our time, developments by its relevance to which the effectiveness and value of the whole legal order will be judged. Each of them involves the addition of a major new chapter to the law: the international law of corporations, the international law of ultra-hazardous liability, and the international law of public actions for the defence of human rights. These are, in themselves, legal technicalities, but they are legal technicalities which are directly related to the fundamental problems of our society: the precarious equilibrium of law and force, the interplay of law, politics and economics, the interplay of law, science and technology, and the interplay of law, morality and humanity.

A generation ago international law was still widely regarded as a 'law between states only and exclusively'.[2] Today it has clearly passed beyond that phase. The increasingly complex pattern of international life has been reflected by the development during the past century of an ever-increasing variety of forms of associative action on an international scale. A large number of official international bodies has been established by states or their governments, or as subsidiary agencies of existing international bodies, to discharge governmental functions of interest to a number of countries; some of these have been established, with varying degrees of autonomy, within the United Nations system, others are independent inter-governmental organisations, others are regional

[1] *Ibid.*, 677.   [2] Oppenheim, *International Law*, 1905, p. 341.

bodies. What are in essence official international trust funds have been established by states and by official international organisations. There already exist a number of international public corporations analogous to the public corporations created in many countries for the control of nationalised services and industries and further developments of this nature seem highly probable. International bodies corporate have been created by states and inter-governmental organisations for the promotion of cultural, educational, medical, scientific and charitable purposes. Innumerable international associations for the pursuit of a wide variety of scientific, cultural, philanthropic and similar ends have been constituted by private initiative and secured varying degrees of recognition from governments and official international bodies. A number of privately established trust funds have in some respects an international character. Interest groups have organised themselves internationally into bodies such as the various international trade union federations and the numerous international trade associations. Developments in the organisation of industry and commerce have resulted in the growth of combines and cartels the interests and connections of which are distributed over many different countries. Multiple incorporation devices have made possible what are in effect international corporations for profit-making purposes. An increasing interest has been shown in the possibility of creating international or European companies with a distinctive status as such. This teeming luxuriance of forms of international associative action has posed a wide range of new problems which cannot be resolved within the framework of a law 'which altereth not'.

The importance and variety of these problems may be illustrated in two distinct areas of intensive development, the world of official international bodies and the world of international economic life, corresponding broadly to the field of government and that of industry and commerce.

As recently as the mid-1940s, at the time of the creation of the United Nations and the reconstitution or creation of the various specialised agencies, the nature and extent of the corporate personality and legal capacity which could and should be conferred upon such bodies was the subject of much hesitation and debate. The outcome was the clear establishment, primarily by a whole series of constituent instruments, general conventions on immunities, and headquarters' agreements,[1] of the principle that such bodies have, for municipal and international purposes alike, the legal capacities of bodies corporate, distinct from their

[1] *Cf.* C. W. Jenks, *International Immunities*, Stevens and Sons, 1961.

membership and subject to the control of their membership only in accordance with the terms of their own constitutions.

The implication of this new status for municipal law purposes presented some novel problems, chiefly as regards the law applicable to the transactions of such bodies.[1] In the main its effect was to give them a recognisable and clearly defined legal status governed by existing law. The question was important chiefly in respect of matters such as property and contract their legal rights concerning which, previously uncertain and precarious, had become a matter of much greater practical significance as a result of the new scale and increasingly operational character of their activities.

The implications of this new status for international law purposes presented problems of a wholly different nature. There was no recognised international law of bodies corporate. What were the implications of the emergence alongside states of a new category or series of categories of international entities for the whole structure of the international legal system? In what sense and to what extent were these new entities subjects of international law and what were the practical results of their recognition as such? How far, and with what modifications, could their relations with each other and with states be regarded as governed by international law? How far did they enjoy capacity to conclude agreements governed by international law? How far did they possess, or could they and should they be granted, a *locus standi in judicio* before international courts and tribunals? What capacity did they or should they enjoy to maintain their rights by bringing international claims in other ways? What right of access to each other, and participation in each others' proceedings, should they enjoy? How far did they or should they possess the active and passive rights of legation or something analogous thereto? How were they affected by the benefit and burden of general international conventions? To what extent should the immunities derived from their international status go beyond jurisdictional immunity and include exemption from inapplicable or inappropriate substantive legal requirements? How was the law governing their corporate life, their relations with their members, and the mutual relations of their organs and agents, to be determined? What measure of financial liability for corporate obligations rested upon the members of such bodies? What rights of action in respect of obligations towards such bodies as corporate entities could be exercised by the members of such bodies in their

[1] *Cf.* C. W. Jenks, *The Proper Law of International Organisations*, Stevens and Sons, 1962.

individual capacities or in the form of a representative action or *actio populationis*?

It was clear from the outset that none of these problems could be resolved within the framework of a law 'which altereth not'. Many of them have been considerably elucidated by the developments of the last twenty years, but none has been finally resolved, and in respect of all of them the process of gradually evolving a body of law appropriate to contemporary needs continues. In the *Reparations for Injuries suffered in the Service of the United Nations Case* the International Court established unequivocally the principle that the United Nations has the capacity to bring an international claim in respect of injuries suffered by persons in its service. The decision, which states clearly that the United Nations is 'an international person' which is 'a subject of international law and capable of possessing international rights and duties'[1] is rightly regarded as a landmark in the recognition of the corporate personality of the United Nations and the independence of the United Nations and its agents from national authority and control, but it sketches a principle rather than determines its applications. The determination of the precise scope of the principle, both as regards the types of injury or damage which it covers and as regards the range of bodies to which it applies, remains a task for the future. In the *Effect of Awards of Compensation Made by the United Nations Administrative Tribunal Case* the Court held that the financial obligations of the United Nations are not qualified by the budgetary powers of the General Assembly.[2] In this case also, however, the principle leaves unanswered important questions concerning its scope and the modalities of its application. What if activities have been undertaken *ultra vires* or without proper authority and financial obligations have been incurred in connection therewith? How far are such obligations binding upon the Organisation and its members? In the *Certain Expenses of the United Nations Case* the Court recognised that 'both national and international law contemplate cases in which the body corporate or public may be bound, as to third parties, by the *ultra vires* act of an agent'[3] but Sir Gerald Fitzmaurice expressed in his concurring opinion doubt concerning the scope of the principle.[4] The problem of the rights of action of members of corporate bodies in respect of obligations towards such bodies in their corporate capacity has been posed rather than resolved by the decision of the Court in the *Northern Cameroons Case*[5] that it was unnecessary to pronounce upon the matter

---

[1] 1949 I.C.J. 174. [2] 1954 I.C.J. 59. [3] 1962 I.C.J. 168.
[4] *Ibid.*, 199–200. [5] 1963 I.C.J. 15.

in that case, the inconsistent decisions given by changed majorities at successive phases of the *South West Africa Case*[1], and the widely divergent concurring and dissenting judgments in all of these cases. Save for the formulation of broad principle in the *Reparation for Injuries Case* judicial exposition has foreshadowed the problems rather than resolved them. They remain problems which cannot be resolved within the framework of a law 'which altereth not'.

As we pass from the field of government to that of industry and commerce we encounter similar problems at a somewhat earlier stage of development. We find that the interplay between nationalist politics and economic entities with world-wide interests and responsibilities cannot be accommodated within the traditional pattern of public international law, the conflict of laws and national legal systems. This inherited trichotomy of the legal order cannot cope with the international economic order which the thrust and ingenuity of commercial enterprise have created. Economic life is now of a complexity, and involves a degree of world-wide interdependence, which defies any possibility of rational control, international or national, on the basis of existing legal systems. The problem takes different forms in respect of different industries, branches of commerce and forms of transport, and in relation to countries varying widely in their existing and potential resources and stages of present and prospective economic development, but there are significant contexts in which it is difficult to conceive of the problem being solved without the creation of some new international regime and status for economic concerns engaged in worldwide operations.

In Iran you have had a body of experience in the petroleum industry which may have a significant bearing on the wider problem. The ingenious provisions of the Consortium Agreement of 1954, with the Iranian Government and the National Oil Company as the parties of the one side and a consortium of eight companies registered in four different countries as the parties of the other side, with agent companies registered as Dutch but subject to the supervision of the National Oil Company of Iran as the means of conducting extraction and refining operations in Iran, and with commercial companies registered in Iran by each of the members of the consortium to fulfil its obligations relating to the export and sale of oil, demonstrate the fertility of resource which may be necessary in developing new legal devices to meet new needs. The 1957 joint partnership agreements provide still another formula. One cannot exclude the possibility that further developments may take place through

[1] 1962 I.C.J. 319; 1966 I.C.J. 6.

some form of cooperation between the Organisation of Petroleum Exporting Countries and international economic interests.

In relation to aviation, river development, power grids, plants using advanced technology, space satellite systems, insurance and other fields the problem assumes a somewhat different form, but its characteristic elements are constant. No national law can effectively control multinational corporations. Conversely, multi-national corporations cannot operate effectively within a recognised legal framework if they are subject to the uncoordinated control of a large number of states, each concerned primarily with its own national interests. A world of some 130, and perhaps soon 150, separate states needs multi-national corporations for the management of an increasing range of common economic interests and services. An international regime and status for such corporations— with the regulation implied in the regime and the privileges attached to the status correlative to each other—has therefore become indispensable. The scope and urgency of the problem have been aptly described by a recent Lebanese writer:

> No one national state is in a position to exercise adequate powers of control, review or coordination over an increasing number of international corporations whose operations transcend national boundaries and even natural barriers between continents. Major oil combines, for example, possess such an internationally integrated and regulated system of operations, such a wealth of assets and investments, such a high annual income, that they approach the status of 'independent economic states' with de facto sovereignty . . . With the absence of international legal control over international corporations and combines, national law remains the only law available in theory to exercise such control. Unfortunately, this law is largely ineffective beyond the territorial boundaries of the state. Multi-national operations cannot be adequately regulated by any single national law. Furthermore, the national state often finds itself confronted with a corporation that is economically its equal or even superior, and political power proves an ineffective weapon to use against economic power. . . . The challenge of the unrestricted expansion of economic power induced national legal systems to develop a whole new branch of law to regulate economic and business activities. . . . Although internationally operating corporations are generally far more powerful than domestic companies, and hence possess the ability to spread the harmful concentration of economic power across the boundaries of many nations,

international law has so far failed to develop in such a way as to meet the need to which national law already responded.[1]

Neither a solution which denies national claims nor a solution conceived in purely national terms can resolve these difficulties. There is therefore a real coincidence of interest between states and multi-national corporations in the establishment of a new international regime and status for such corporations.

It is not my purpose here to offer any solution for the problem, but merely to emphasise how vividly it illustrates the impossibility of resolving the fundamental problems of the interplay of law, politics and economics in the world community of tomorrow within the framework of a law 'which altereth not'.

When we turn from the interplay of law, politics and economics to that of law, science and technology we are confronted with essentially the same situation. The contemporary progress of science and technology has completely changed man's relationship to his natural environment. Aviation, air and water pollution, nuclear energy, activities in space, earth-probing, weather and climate modification schemes, cybernetic developments, and biological experiments have created a wide range of known and unknown hazards for which the law as we inherited it made no adequate provision. We are in the earliest stages of developing an appropriate body of law governing these matters. Some of the fundamental principles involved are becoming clear. They derive from the common interest of mankind in ensuring that the hazards of scientific and technological innovation and of continuing ultra-hazardous activities are equitably born and do not fall upon their chance victim, and that such innovations and activities do not destroy, disrupt, disintegrate or pollute the natural environment on which human life and welfare depend or release forces having such a tendency which are liable to escape from human control. They include the obligation of every state to cooperate in preventive measures for the avoidance of known and foreseeable hazards from ultra-hazardous activities in accordance with appropriate international conventions and regulations; the obligation to participate in procedures of consultation and inquiry before authorising action involving unknown hazards; and the obligation to avoid, or failing avoidance to indemnify, injury from ultra-hazardous activities to the world community or to other states or their nationals. To make these

---

[1] M. A. Mughraby, *Permanent Sovereignty Over Oil Resources: A Study of Middle East Oil Concessions and Legal Change*, Beirut, 1966, pp. 164–6.

principles practically effective a wide range of questions concerning the substitution of risk for fault, financial security for the discharge of ultra-hazardous liability, the relationship of civil and international liability, and other matters must be resolved.[1] None of them can be resolved within the framework of a law 'which altereth not'. The successful negotiation just announced of a treaty providing for the enjoyment of space and the celestial bodies by all mankind, the demilitarisation of the moon and other celestial bodies, and the denuclearisation of space and all the celestial bodies is a major step in this general direction. It is important that it should give an impetus to further progress.

Equally without directly applicable precedent is the problem of how far a state may act beyond its jurisdiction to protect itself against the consequences of ultra-hazardous activities. A nuclear or space disaster, or the pollution problem arising from the wreckage of a great tanker, may create a need for action which is 'instant' and 'overwhelming' but nevertheless leaves some 'choice of means' and a brief 'moment for deliberation'[2] which, with the benefit of modern communications, may afford some opportunity of consultation. The problem calls for thorough and urgent review but cannot be resolved within the framework of a law 'which altereth not'.

When we proceed to consider the interplay of law, morality and humanity the position proves to be essentially the same as in respect of law, politics and economics and law, science and technology. The extent to which states have a legal interest in the performance of an international obligation to promote the general welfare became the issue on which the International Court of Justice divided equally (but for the casting vote of the President) in the *South West Africa Case*, but the decision in that case deals with the matter only in the specific and highly special context of the mandate for South West Africa. The more general question remains open. As the dissenting opinions in that case make so abundantly clear,[3] there is an imposing body of international precedent for such a legal interest, covering fields as diverse as slavery, minorities, dependent peoples, labour, genocide, racial discrimination and human

[1] I have attempted to explore these problems more fully in 'Liability for Ultra-hazardous Activities in International Law', *Recueil des Cours de l'Académie de Droit international*, vol. 117, 1966 (I), pp. 101–198.
[2] The reference is to Daniel Webster's definition, with reference to the *Caroline Case* of 1837, of the circumstances justifying the violation of the territory of another state for the purposes of self-defence; cf. Jenks, *The Common Law of Mankind*, 1958, p. 141.
[3] Judge Wellington Koo, at 1966 I.C.J., 226–8; Judge Tanaka, *ibid.*, 252; Judge Jessup, *ibid.*, 373–85.

rights generally, and there are a number of existing international procedures, such as those established by the Constitution of the International Labour Organisation, which clearly confer a legal interest in the
general welfare on states not directly involved. If any substantial progress is to be made in the international protection of human rights the
concept of the general welfare as a legal interest will require much fuller
consideration and present a wide range of new problems, none of which
can be resolved within the framework of a law 'which altereth not'.

The need for such progress is one of the overriding preoccupations of
our time. As His Majesty the Shahanshah said yesterday in his Human
Rights Day Message, 'Political rights without social justice, and political
democracy without economic democracy, cannot bring about the true
aspirations of the people of any society' and the resulting problem must
be tackled on a world scale. 'The achievement of human rights in one
country or in one part of the world is not enough. Human society has
become so deeply involved in one another's fate that the violation of part
or all of these rights in one society is reflected in all.' Sa'di expressed the
same thought: 'The sons of Adam are limbs of each other, having been
created of one essence.'[1] We cannot give adequate expression to the
conscience of mankind in respect of issues involving the freedom and
dignity of man within the framework of a law 'which altereth not'.

Once we have discarded the mythology of a law 'which altereth not'
we must come to grips with the fundamental question of the metabolism
of the law, the manner in which law grows by absorbing into itself, by
recognised processes, elements originally extraneous to the legal system.
In all three of the major fields which we have reviewed, the relationship
of law, politics and economics, the relationship of law, science and
technology, and the relationship of law, morality and humanity, this is
the core of the problem.

The majority decision of the International Court of Justice counsels
caution in the matter. The Court, the judgment tells us:

> . . . is a court of law and can take account of moral principles only in
> so far as these are given a sufficient expression in legal form. Law
> exists, it is said, to serve a social need; but precisely for that reason it
> can do so only through and within the limits of its own discipline.
> Otherwise, it is not a legal service that will be rendered.

Humanitarian considerations 'may constitute the inspirational basis for

[1] *The Gulistan of Sa'di*, I, 10, translated by Edward Rehatsek, Allen and
Unwin, 1964, at p. 85.

E

rules of law' but 'do not, however, in themselves amount to rules of law'. The existence of an interest 'does not of itself entail that this interest is specifically juridical in character'. In order to generate legal rights and obligations 'the interest must be given juridical expression and be clothed in legal form'.[1]

From these general propositions, expressed with this degree of generality, no self-respecting lawyer will dissent, but they leave wholly unanswered the questions presented by their application to any particular case. What constitutes 'a sufficient expression in legal form'? Where does the law draw 'the limits of its own discipline'? When does an interest become 'specifically juridical in character'? On these questions there may be, and are, wide divergences of view. When the law is confronted with substantive and methodological problems of this order of importance, how can it, while remaining faithful to the traditions of legal method necessary to its continued authority as a legal order, keep pace with the changing and growing substantive needs of society?

There are of course some who take the view that the task is inherently impossible, that the revolutionary forces of society have shattered its legal framework, and that no stable legal order enjoying general confidence can be recreated without a fresh start. How it is then to be created, in an agglomeration of perhaps 150 independent and disparate states each claiming that its consent is necessary to the validity of any legal rule, is far from apparent. An evolutionary approach is clearly preferable, but is possible only on the basis of general confidence that the law is being reshaped to meet new needs by orderly processes but with a sustained vigour corresponding to the scale and urgency of these needs. We can neither maintain nor expand the rule of law without a frank recognition of the magnitude and novelty of the problems for which established precedent affords no answer and a clear willingness to use boldly the creative potentialities of a growing legal system to resolve these problems in the spirit of the age.

What are the respective parts in this process of growth, development and change of the continued vitality of custom (evolved increasingly by collective international action rather than by the concurrent but uncoordinated action of individual states), of international legislative action, and of international adjudication? To analyse these in any detail is a task for a more leisurely occasion. Meanwhile it must suffice to emphasise that all three play vital and mutually complementary parts. Without the continued vitality of custom we lose the necessary link between law and

[1] 1966 I.C.J. 34.

the daily practice of states and international organisations which corresponds to the manner in which law has always grown out of the current usage of society. Without improved processes of international legislation we cannot hope to make reasonably expeditiously necessary changes in the law which go beyond the margin of more gradual change afforded by changing custom and the continuous reappraisal of the law by the developing jurisprudence of international courts and tribunals. The prevailing temper of international adjudication may nevertheless be almost decisive in determining whether or not the law responds effectively to the changing challenges of society.

Judicial innovation may be full of perils but a static law cannot hold the allegiance of a dynamic society. 'A judicial innovation', Sir Gerald Fitzmaurice has written, 'is too dearly purchased if it is made at the sacrifice of the integrity of the law.'[1] Thus far there can be no dissent; but integrity does not imply immobility, and the measure in which a particular change in the law threatens the integrity of the legal system is always a difficult question of judgment involving factors not all of which are exclusively legal. A legal system in which the judicial process is irresponsive to the groundswell of the world convulsion of our time cannot fulfil the primary function of providing an orderly framework for inevitable social change. You will, I trust, forgive me if I conclude by reverting from the Iranian to the Hellenic tradition and quoting Heraclitus: 'Everything flows'. That salutary maxim holds the key to an expanding rule of law in an organised world community. We need a 'white revolution' developing insistently the law as we have inherited it into an accepted and effective common law of mankind.

[1] *Cambridge Essays in International Law: Essays in Honour of Lord McNair,* Stevens and Sons, 1965, p. 47.

5

Law and the pursuit of peace[1]

The pursuit of peace is the major challenge of our time. The part which law can play in the pursuit of peace is the largest question confronting international lawyers at this or any time. It is not a new question; it has been a brooding presence in the law from its earliest days; but it remains an unresolved question, and it assumes new forms with successive changes in the complexion of world affairs.

Peace is being, and will continue to be, sought in many different ways: by power, by diplomacy, by economic and social policy, by education and by international organisation. It must and will continue to be sought in all these ways; but in none of these ways can peace be made secure on a continuing basis without the use of law as one of the necessary instruments for the purpose. Law alone can bring us no peace; but without law neither faith nor works can resolve the problems, or meet the needs, of society; in this respect the world community is no different from every other form of society known to man. Policy and morality are as important constituents of world order as legality; but without legality policy is apt to become arbitrary and morality subjective. It is for this fundamental reason that countless generations of wise men have regarded respect for the rule of law as the foundation of sound policy and the heart of political morality. So it is within the state, and so it is in world affairs. There are, however, certain fundamental conditions which must be fulfilled by any legal system which aspires to play a significant part on the world stage in the pursuit of peace. First, it must be a law for the whole world—what I have ventured to call elsewhere the common law of mankind.[2] An international law which is but Roman law writ large, with a dash of empiricism derived from the common law tradition, lacks sufficiently broad and deep foundations to impose itself upon the seething world of today. We need, and we are evolving, a

[1] An address to a joint meeting of the Indian Society of International Law and the Indian Branch of the International Law Association, New Delhi, 6 January 1965.
[2] *The Common Law of Mankind*, 1958.

common law which represents a synthesis of the legal traditions of all mankind, of which we can say with the fullest truth in Lord Stowell's classical phrase that 'the law itself has no locality' but embodies the aspirations and satisfies the sense of justice of free men everywhere, irrespective of differences in their inherited cultures and the legal systems in which they were born and bred. This is not a dream for the future; it is the daily round of today. We have in the varied legal systems of the world a sufficient consensus on the fundamentals of the law of peace to build the common law of mankind; to build that law is the day by day task of the contemporary international lawyer.

Secondly, the law must be a law of freedom and welfare.[1] It must, of course, secure for the world community peace, order and good government; but these are the foundations rather than the whole purpose of world order. The world community of today reflects the responsibilities and preoccupations of the modern state; it seeks the good life for all its peoples and judges the adequacy of its law by its social purposes as a community.

Thirdly, the law must be a law for a dynamic society. The world has changed more in our time than throughout the whole of previous recorded history; the rate of change is still accelerating and its scope ever widening. We cannot imprison this process of change in legal traditions which have lost the breath of life. The law is an essential element in the continuity of the social order, but in order to remain effective as such it must constantly justify itself anew; it is particularly important that it should remain effective as such an element of continuity, and continuously justify itself anew for this purpose, in a world in which the social order has been so violently disrupted in so many places that the most crucial of all problems is to rescue the peaceful evolution of society from the prospect of utter chaos. Only a dynamic law can preserve the rule of law in a dynamic society.

Within the context of this general philosophy we can identify certain primary functions which the law must fulfil:

it must protect the common peace;
it must promote the common welfare;
in order to protect the common peace, the law must—
    debar recourse to armed force save in the common interest;
    regulate armament under the control of the community;
    provide safeguards against escalation into war;

[1] *Cf.* C. W. Jenks, *Law, Freedom and Welfare*, Stevens and Sons, 1963.

make effective provision for the peaceful settlement of international disputes; and

embody the principle of mutual aid to restrain acts of aggression
and maintain or restore international peace and security.

In order to promote the common welfare, the law must—

protect human rights;

grant fullness of opportunity;

provide a legal framework for economic stability and growth; and

stimulate, guide and harness scientific and technological progress
for the common good.

What do these postulates of the effectiveness of international law
imply? It has been said that Mr Justice Holmes regarded the imposition
of group norms upon individuals as 'the basic overhead cost of life lived
as social beings'.[1] What, in terms of the contribution which we must
exact from the law, is the minimum 'basic overhead cost' of the peace
and progress of the world community? Let us consider each postulate
in turn.

The law must debar recourse to armed force save in the common
interest. It already does so: the Charter of the United Nations is unequivocal on the subject. The obligation of members to refrain in their
international relations from the threat or use of force in any manner
inconsistent with the purposes of the United Nations is absolute. Without such an obligation the prospect of maintaining world peace by more
effective international organisation becomes altogether illusory. No
ideological qualification of the obligation can be regarded as acceptable.
Any attempt to import such a qualification into the obligation will
inevitably so destroy the obligation itself as to defeat the purposes of
those who seek to qualify it. The concept that the obligation cannot be
invoked to restrain those chafing against injustice by the continuing
aggression of a colonial, post-colonial or neo-colonial regime not only
misstates the problem; it makes both the problem of peace and the
problem of justice wholly impossible of solution. The obligation
becomes meaningless and inoperative if we allow it to be qualified by
anything other than the necessary right of individual and collective
self-defence, reasonably construed and subject to impartial review. The
Charter of the United Nations will inevitably lose its political, its legal,
and its moral authority unless we are prepared to discharge in full the
obligations which it implies for ourselves.

[1] J. W. Hurst, *Justice Holmes on Legal History*, Collier-Macmillan, 1964,
p. 102.

The law must regulate armament under the control of the community. No legal system which fails to discipline the armed strength of its over-mighty subjects can hope to maintain authority or provide an adequate basis for peace, order and good government. International law has not yet succeeded in fulfilling this function. History records many examples of the unilateral disarmament of defeated enemies, but such arrangements are in their nature transitory. Of demilitarised zones there have also been many examples, but only the unarmed frontier between the United States and Canada has a long and significant history. Only in the field of naval disarmament were there for a time, during the inter-war period, effective agreements to which the leading naval powers were parties; in retrospect these agreements still have a lasting historical importance by reason of their having eliminated the danger of naval rivalry between the United Kingdom and the United States during a crucial phase in the readjustment of their relative strength and mutual relations, but they are more often judged and condemned as having impaired instead of establishing the balance of power in the Pacific. There have also been a series of mutual renunciations of weapons which successive stages in the attitude of public opinion to new technologies have condemned as barbarous, from the poisoning of arrows and wells to submarine, gas and germ warfare; these have not, as is so often assumed, been wholly ineffective, but their effect has tended to be limited and has always been precarious.

Since 1919 there have been, except for the period of the Second World War and the years immediately preceding it, virtually continuous though constantly interrupted negotiations for disarmament under effective international control. The problem has changed greatly in character in the course of the last fifty years by reason of the changed anatomy of world politics and the impact of advanced technology on the art of war. In the relations of nuclear powers, nuclear weapons, long-range delivery systems and the possibility of the military use of space have given minutes the military significance of months or years in the days of more conventional weapon systems and strategy. These new factors have shifted the emphasis of the problem of verification from controls designed to ensure that conventional armed strength cannot be built up gradually in such a manner as to disrupt the balance of strength provided for in the disarmament agreement without what is taking place becoming generally known, to controls designed to ensure that advanced technology cannot be applied without warning to military ends. We have moved from the limitation of the number of warships, bombers and trained reserves to the detection of nuclear tests, the control of fissile material and missile sites, and the demilitarisation of space. This is a far more complex task. It calls for a more sophisticated skill in negotiating the necessary international agreements. We cannot escape the difficulties of the problem by over-simplifying it and calling for measures of disarmament unaccompanied by any effective protection of good faith. Unless we are all prepared to accept and discharge the obligations of a series of agreements covering these fields which provide for comprehensive measures of disarmament policed by effective measures of verification and control, the law will remain unable to police its over-mighty subjects; there will be no arms control and no peace.

The law must provide safeguards against escalation into war. It cannot ignore small wars on the ground that they do not in themselves involve any immediate danger of nuclear peril. It cannot afford to assume that what happens in the high Pamirs or in the jungles of South-East Asia or Central Africa lies beyond its concern. It cannot treat civil strife, in the sands of Araby or in ancient islands off the Trojan shore, as beyond the purview of the international community. A vacuum of orderly government has always been a threat to the peace. There is, however, no more difficult problem in the present phase of development of international organisation than that of defining, organising and financing the part which military and civilian operations by international organisations should play in averting the breakdown of normal processes of government in situations of instability and civil strife in which the primary responsibility of a national government has to be supplemented by international action through the United Nations. Unless we are all prepared to play our part in clarifying and developing the law on the subject, and to accept and discharge the political, military and financial obligations which may be involved, the stability of international relations will remain permanently at the mercy of the instability of the least stable members of the international community.

The law must make effective provision for the peaceful settlement of international disputes. The method of settlement may to some extent vary with circumstances. As the Charter recognises, negotiation, inquiry, mediation, arbitration, judicial settlement, resort to regional arrangements or agencies and other peaceful means all have distinctive parts to play. But among these methods only judicial settlement based on the compulsory jurisdiction of international courts and tribunals gives any assurance of a decision formally binding upon the parties. The other methods are devices for promoting agreement rather than procedures for

securing a decision. The part which judicial settlement can play effectively in any particular context is admittedly limited by the attitude of
the parties and the extent to which they are prepared to accept a settlement based on the judicial application of a growing but still in many
respects somewhat indeterminate body of law. The content of the law
and the content of international relations at any particular time and the
general posture of international politics at that time may operate as
limiting factors. But unless we are all prepared to play our part in
promoting the wider acceptance of judicial settlement and to accept
a substantial measure of compulsory jurisdiction as the cornerstone of
an expanding rule of law, our status as protagonists of the peaceful
settlement of international disputes will remain equivocal.

The law must embody the principle of mutual aid to restrain acts of
aggression and maintain or restore international peace and security. It
already does so. The maintenance of international peace and security by
measures including effective collective measures for the prevention and
removal of threats to the peace and for the suppression of acts of aggression or other breaches of the peace is set forth in the Charter as the first
and foremost of the purposes of the United Nations. The obligation has
perhaps been obscured by the strains and upheavals of the last twenty
years and the politics of the cold war and non-alignment, but the principle remains as fundamental as it was in the days when the Manchurian,
Ethiopian and Rhineland crises destroyed the prestige and authority of
the League of Nations and left it powerless to prevent the Second World
War. Unless we are all prepared to discharge in full the obligations
relating to peace and security and mutual aid in restraint of aggression
which the Charter implies for ourselves we have no moral standing to
complain of aggression by others or to seek succour in time of need.

The law must protect human rights. We can no longer regard the
protection of civil liberties as being exclusively or essentially within the
domestic jurisdiction of each state. The promotion of universal respect
for, and observance of, human rights and fundamental freedoms for all
raises, in the present stage of development of international relations,
issues so far-reaching for the world as a whole that the law must embrace
them within its purview. We all recognise this instinctively in relation to
states of whose policies we disapprove. We are all reluctant to admit it
in relation to ourselves or to concede that our own policies and practices
need, or should be subject to, any external appraisal or review. Our conviction that sovereignty is not enough stops at the waterfront. Within
our own ramparts we still reject the right of appeal to the conscience of

mankind. In this respect we are, I fear, all pretty much alike. But there can be no double, triple or other multiple standard in these matters. An effective world charter of human rights and effective procedures for its implementation presuppose a general willingness to recognise that none of us can remain the final judge of his own fulfilment of our common obligation to respect human rights and fundamental freedoms for all, without distinction as to race, sex, language or religion. The United Nations Covenants of Human Rights will, if they are widely and promptly ratified without reservations which detract significantly from the obligations which they embody, and if the procedures of implementation for which they provide are applied with thoroughness and objectivity, constitute such a charter; but they will be ineffective unless we are all prepared to accept the obligations which they would imply for ourselves.

The law must grant fullness of opportunity. The Charter of the United Nations embodies a pledge of mutual cooperation in the promotion of higher standards of living, full employment, and conditions of economic and social progress and development. The pledge has already been translated into far-reaching modifications of policies. The world now recognises a collective responsibility for the common welfare which is the international counterpart of the modern conception of the welfare state. But for the most part collective action for economic advancement still rests on a precarious basis of spontaneous cooperation. It remains at the mercy of political uncertainty and changing political views. While all the technical cooperation programmes of the United Nations rest on the basis of annual pledges of voluntary contributions, there is no assurance that collective action for economic and social advancement will remain continuously effective. No other basis for such programmes is, however, conceivable until new forms of cooperation between highly developed and developing countries based on a consensus resting on common interests have been evolved. It is in this general spirit that a firmer framework of mutual obligation must be sought. There can be no great society on the world scale unless we are all prepared to accept the obligations which a fuller recognition of the collective interest in the common welfare would imply for ourselves. These obligations embrace fullness of opportunity within as well as among nations. No state has a moral claim to international aid for its development unless it assures fullness of opportunity to its own citizens. The continued willingness of the advanced countries to contribute to international social justice may well depend on the extent to which international social justice is translated everywhere into national social justice. In the modern state the law has become more than the foundation and guarantee of public order and private rights; it has, without relinquishing these functions, become also the instrument of the social policy of the community. Many of the dilemmas which confront us in the present stage of the development of the law arise from the needs to reconcile its traditional and newer functions. International law is confronted with a series of similar dilemmas; it cannot hope to resolve them unless we are all prepared to accept the implications for international and national policy alike which the obligations of mutual cooperation embodied in the Charter involve for ourselves.

The law must provide a framework for economic stability and growth. Currency, trade, commodity policy and investment are among the subjects in respect of which it must achieve a reasonable balance of conflicting interests. In matters of currency and trade we are groping our way, by still somewhat unsteady steps, towards obligations of mutual consultation prior to unilateral action affecting common interests, and measures of mutual support for weakened economies as a means of strengthening the economy of the world as a whole. In commodity policy the free play of market forces is tending to be superseded, by even more groping steps, by negotiated arrangements between producers and consumers designed to secure greater stability in production and prices on an equitable basis. In the field of investment we are experimenting in new techniques, including the operations of the International Bank and its affiliates, varied types of consortium, and a wide range of joint ventures, with a view to reconciling the independence of growing economies from control by external political and economic forces and interests with the need for the security of investment without which the outside capital necessary for intensified and accelerated development of an emerging economy in a free society cannot be attracted. The United Nations Conference on Trade and Development has given a powerful stimulus to further action in all these fields. We are now all consciously involved in the establishment and maintenance of equitable terms of trade as the crux of a deliberate policy of intensified and accelerated economic development transcending frontiers and ideologies. None of these economic objectives for which the law must provide a framework can be achieved unless we are all prepared to accept the obligations which they would imply for ourselves.

The law must stimulate, guide and harness scientific and technological progress for the common good. In a wide range of fields, of which aviation and telecommunications are examples, international rules have

become necessary as the basis of key international services. The Partial
Nuclear Test Ban Treaty and the Treaty on Principles Governing the
Activities of States in the Exploration and Use of Outer Space, including
the Moon and Other Celestial Bodies, are but the opening chapters of
the international law of advanced technology. Nuclear energy and space
exploration are only the most dramatic of the many developments which
are transforming man's relationship to his natural environment in a
manner which makes it urgent to develop a further body of law to govern
experiments with the unknown which may determine the whole future
of man. We shall succeed in bridging divergent views on these matters
only if we start from the twin assumptions that we are all potential
partners in the scientific and technological adventure of our times and all
potential victims of scientific and technological misadventure; if some of
us assume that we are primarily potential partners, and others that we
are primarily potential victims, there will be no consensus on such
matters as the legality of space experiments and liability for damage
resulting from nuclear or space activities. The common interest in a
reasonable equilibrium of freedom and control will involve important
obligations for us all.[1] We cannot so develop the law as to ensure that
nuclear energy and space are used for exclusively peaceful purposes
unless we are all prepared to accept the obligations which a self-denying
ordinance on the subject accompanied by effective measures of international control would imply for ourselves.

I have postulated ambitious targets for the law. But I have not invited
you to indulge the idle fancies of a dreamer. To achieve these targets we
will need a full measure of practical idealism, but all of them reflect the
daily preoccupations of practical men. Unless we set our sights high, we
cannot hope for a breakthrough towards the rule of law in world affairs.
We seek such a breakthrough towards the rule of law in world affairs,
not as lawyers seeking a future for the law, but as practical men concerned with the future of society. We are, all of us, however widely our
traditions and upbringing may differ, the children of a continuing revolution, which has in our lifetimes transformed politics, strategy, economics, social structures and cultural values, and opened up new scientific
and technological possibilities, throughout, and indeed beyond, the
world. The world cannot long continue to hover between endemic chaos
and the prospect of mutual annihilation precariously restrained by a

---

[1] *Cf.* Jenks, 'Liability for Ultra-hazardous Activities in International Law',
Recueil des Cours de l'Académie de Droit international, vol. 117, 1966 (I),
pp. 101–198.

balance of terror. Man has deserved better than this as the fruit of his endless adventure in quest of peace and security, justice, freedom and welfare. We live in a changed world which calls for a dynamic approach to new problems. None of us finds it easy to discard inhibitions and intellectual habits and predilections which represent the conditioned reflexes of a world which we have now outgrown. But none of us can escape from an obligation which rests upon us all. Only by discarding the prejudices of the past can we survive the vibrant challenge of the present and enjoy the boundless promise of the future. We need a new lease of intellectual vitality; we need a renewed sense of moral purpose; we need a new iron of resolve to expand the frontiers of freedom and widen the horizons of opportunity. Let us build together the common law of mankind as an essential element in the institutional embodiment and foundation of the ideal of human unity. Let us mould the common law of mankind as a response to Tagore's great prayer:

Where the mind is without fear and the head is held high;
Where knowledge is free;
Where the world has not been broken into fragments by narrow
    domestic walls;
Into that heaven of freedom

Let mankind awake.

6

Mutual aid in international law[1]

Mutual aid is among the most civilising influences of any human society. Anthropologists, sociologists and comparative lawyers have traced the part which it has played in the evolution of social and legal institutions in diverse cultures and across the centuries. The anthropologists have assembled evidence on the subject which gives a picture of primitive society sharply contrasting with that of Hobbes; among the field studies made in India I have found the account of mutual aid in agriculture given by Grigson *The Maria Gonds of Bastar*[2] particularly interesting. Among sociologists Kropotkin was, of course, the pioneer, and remains the leading authority; he finds in mutual aid among animals, mutual aid among savages, mutual aid among the barbarians who overran the Roman Empire, and mutual aid in the medieval city, the antecedents of mutual aid among ourselves;[3] in mutual aid among ourselves he finds the key to the future of mankind and the 'best guarantee of still loftier evolution of our race'.[4] Among lawyers, Maine and Vinogradoff discussed the concept as one of the germinal ideas of ancient jurisprudence; Maine pointed out that one of the essential purposes of Indian customary law was to secure 'the interdependence and mutual responsibility of the members of an Indian village community';[5] Vinogradoff depicted the joint family system of ancient Aryan law as essentially an experiment in social solidarity and cooperative action.[6] While the village community and the joint family have been profoundly modified by the impact of a market economy and the progress of industrialisation and urbanisation, the fundamental concepts which they embodied remain a part of your

[1] An address to the Madras State Unit of the Indian Law Institute, 4 January 1965.
[2] *The Maria Gonds of Bastar*, Oxford U.P., 1949, pp. 125–50.
[3] *Mutual Aid*, 1902, reprinted Penguin Books, 1939.
[4] *Mutual Aid*, p. 234.
[5] H. S. Maine, *Village Communities in the East and West*, 7th edn., Murray, 1895, p. 117.
[6] P. Vinogradoff, *Outlines of Historical Jurisprudence*, H. Milford, 1921, Vol. 1, pp. 261–73.

heritage and of ours. This was my impression of the position before I arrived here two days ago for the first time in fifteen years. I was happy to find it confirmed by no less an authority than Ananthanarayanan, C. J., who writes:[1]

> The core of the *Mitakshara* joint family still survives as a psychological reality, though the institution itself might be dying. As Dr Derrett has observed, 'mutual belonging, mutual responsibility, reinforced and expressed ... still to this date makes what the author of the *Mitakshara* would call "unseparatedness" rather the rule than the exception'.

Mutual aid is no new-fangled nostrum of rootless radicals; it is part of the imperishable tradition of western and eastern civilisation alike; all that is new is the need to extend the range and scope of the concept to correspond to a scale and content of human relationships which now encompass the world and embrace an ever more complex pattern of activities; but the importance and potentialities of the concept in contemporary society go far beyond anything which previous generations could have imagined.

There is perhaps no single general idea which can exercise, and is exercising, so fruitful and fertilising an influence upon contemporary international law as that of mutual aid. Let us examine some of its implications and applications by considering in turn mutual aid for the maintenance of peace and security, mutual aid in law enforcement, mutual aid for economic stability and growth, and mutual aid for scientific and technological progress. Such mutual aid, evolved and practised by consultation and consensus, but requiring for its effectiveness a framework of clear-cut and binding mutual obligations, is fundamental to the contribution to freedom and welfare of the common law of mankind. These varied applications of the principle are, moreover, complementary to each other; a fuller development of mutual aid for economic stability and growth for scientific and technological progress would certainly be facilitated by, and may be found to be impracticable without, further progress in mutual aid for the maintenance of peace and security and in law enforcement. In all of these contexts the principle is now widely accepted; but in all of them its practical application presents formidable problems which constitute one of the leading challenges of our time to the wisdom of statesmen and the resourcefulness of international lawyers.

[1] *The Hindu*, 3 January 1965.

MUTUAL AID FOR THE MAINTENANCE OF PEACE AND SECURITY

Mutual aid for the maintenance of peace and security is the heart of the Charter of the United Nations as it was the heart of the Covenant of the League of Nations. The maintenance of international peace and security is, by the terms of the Charter, the first and foremost of the purposes of the United Nations; the measures envisaged by the Charter for the purpose include 'effective collective measures for the prevention and removal of threats to the peace and for the suppression of acts of aggression or other breaches of the peace'. The failure of the League of Nations to fulfil its corresponding mandate destroyed the League as a political force and precipitated the Second World War.

In recent years the relationship between the principle of mutual aid for the maintenance of peace and security and the policy of non-alignment has become an issue of primary importance; there is no incompatibility between them. The principle of mutual aid is one of the permanent foundations of international society; without it the common peace will always be precarious. It neither presupposes, nor in itself precludes, alignment. Conversely, non-alignment does not preclude mutual aid against aggression; if it were construed as so doing it would cease to be non-alignment and become a policy of condoning violent disruption of the common peace. Whatever confusion of thought there may have been in the matter, and it appears to have existed in aligned and non-aligned countries alike, is the outcome of failure to appreciate that the two concepts operate on different planes of thought and action and are relevant at different stages in the handling of international conflict. The policy of non-alignment is a legitimate refusal to pledge support in advance to either party to a potential international conflict; it does not imply continued neutrality in the event of aggression in violation of the Charter of the United Nations; it neither debars the non-aligned country from supporting the victim of such aggression nor precludes it if itself the victim from accepting or seeking the support of aligned countries. Conversely, alignment is a legitimate exercise of the right of collective self-defence acknowledged by the Charter; it seeks to minimise the danger of conflict by making clear the degree of resistance which will be offered to aggression, but does not imply any continued obligation of support for any of the co-aligned countries itself committing aggression in violation of the Charter; any such act of aggression repudiates the purpose and destroys the foundation of the alignment.

Universal non-alignment would of course represent the ideal condition for the full and fair application of the principle of mutual aid by means of a system of collective security in which the merits of each case are judged objectively without prior commitment by any of those concerned; as one of the generation deeply stirred by Woodrow Wilson's protest against entangling alliances, I have every sympathy with this aspiration; but any such aspiration presupposes a confidence in the effectiveness of collective security not yet warranted by experience and a far more complete relaxation of existing international tension than is as yet in sight; in the world of today we must as a practical matter assume the continued coexistence of both rival alignments and non-aligned countries. The principle of mutual aid transcends the differences of tradition, interest and approach which have found expression in these divergences of policy.

You will not expect me to resolve this afternoon dilemmas which the world has been wrestling with for a generation, to produce a magic formula for distilling a common resolve to maintain the peace from a welter of conflicting ideologies and interests or to outline some new plan of economic, financial and military measures for the restraint of aggression which will command wider acceptance and be more effective in practice than any suggested hitherto. The most that I can hope to do is to attempt to formulate some of the principles on the basis of which we can grope our way towards a solution. There are, I venture to submit, four principles upon which we can all agree, whether our countries be aligned or non-aligned and irrespective of how they may be aligned.

The first principle is that aggression in violation of the Charter invariably creates a new situation in which the restraint of such aggression assumes an overriding immediate importance and the common interest in the maintenance of peace and security takes precedence over all other considerations. The second principle is that aid or comfort to an aggressor is a hostile act inconsistent with the Charter which cannot be justified by any arrangements for collective self-defence in virtue of which such aid or comfort is claimed or given. The third principle is that aid or comfort towards the victim of aggression is not a hostile act towards any member of the United Nations and does not constitute an act of alignment or a renunciation of the policy of non-alignment. The fourth principle is that the receipt of aid or comfort by a victim of aggression does not constitute an act of alignment with the source of such aid or comfort.

How are we to translate these four principles into practice? How are we to avoid disagreement concerning their applicability to particular

F

cases destroying or making valueless the principles themselves? A number of measures of collective discipline are clearly necessary to make the principles workable.

The starting-point must be an unqualified recognition that no man can be judge in his own cause. This does not mean that no man may take emergency action in his own defence, in that of his neighbour, or on humanitarian grounds, but it does mean that no man may take such action without simultaneously submitting to impartial review both the merits of the cause and the legitimacy and wisdom of the emergency action. In this respect there has been a great development in accepted standards of practice in recent years; we have virtually reached the stage at which a state taking emergency action puts itself in the wrong if it does not simultaneously submit the matter to the United Nations with a full explanation of the nature of, need for, and proposed limits of the action taken.

When the facts are uncertain or the emotional involvement of the parties makes objective appraisal of the facts difficult, there is a strong case for a prompt international judicial inquiry. Such an inquiry may, and in the most difficult cases involving the greatest danger of war probably will, fail to resolve the issues to the satisfaction of both parties. But, even when it fails to avoid or prevent conflict, such an inquiry may have great value. It may clarify the issues to the point at which third parties no longer have any difficulty in determining where their obligations lie. It may provide a basis for a wider consensus of view in the Security Council or the General Assembly than would otherwise be possible. In other cases, it may, without convincing the potential law-breaker, make clear the strength of the case which he may have to meet and the weight of opposition which he is likely to encounter unless he modifies his claims and policy; it may sometimes have this effect in relation to both parties. A successful inquiry may provide a basis for an agreed settlement or, without finally disposing of the matters at issue, permit of limited agreements or adjustments of policy which relax tension. A state declining such an inquiry should be regarded as creating a strong presumption against itself; international bodies should initiate such inquiries almost as a matter of course in appropriate cases; and precautions should be taken to ensure that they are entrusted to men of world reputation assisted by adequate and competent staff of unimpeachable integrity and that they are conducted with the most scrupulous thoroughness and impartiality by a procedure which ensures full protection for the rights of all parties, provides adequate opportunity for each party to question the evidence and contentions of the other, and leaves no basis for a claim by either party that its views have not been fully heard and weighed. The experiments in propaganda diplomacy by committed diplomats sitting as a commission of inquiry are a political instrument of an altogether different nature; there may be, and no doubt are, legitimate occasions for the use of such commissions, but, not being judicial in composition, temper or procedure, they must be clearly distinguished from international judicial inquiries.

Collective review through the United Nations of the legitimacy of allegedly defensive or humanitarian action and judicial inquiry into facts which have engendered explosive emotion can be effective only in a climate of mutual restraint pending the outcome of such review or inquiry. In the Covenant of the League of Nations the concept of a 'cooling-off' period played a central part. We have rightly thought provision for such a period an inadequate protection against war, and in a world in which annihilation may be a matter of minutes rather than of months, years or decades the concept must clearly take a new form. A sense of proportion becomes the essence of the matter, and the future of mankind lies at the mercy of exhausted patience or a mistake of judgment. The power of reason and the reasonableness of power become our only safeguard; in such circumstances, only a mutuality of interest which has become a partnership can afford any real sense of security.

Within such a framework of collective review, judicial inquiry and measured restraint, the principle of mutual aid becomes the lifeblood of society. While its pulse beats steadily and strongly, the body politic is healthy; when that pulse falters, the whole body politic is threatened with decay. Once we renounce, or fail to respond to, the principle of mutual aid for the maintenance of peace and security, the vital force which sustains the life of the world community ebbs away. Every man for himself and the devil take the hindmost replaces the principle of the common peace, upheld by all for the benefit of all; and who shall say that we shall not be the hindmost?

MUTUAL AID IN LAW ENFORCEMENT

Mutual aid in law enforcement has a twofold connotation in international law. It includes both the mutual aid of states in the enforcement of each other's laws and mutual aid in the enforcement of international decisions.

The mutual aid of states in the enforcement of each other's laws covers a wide range. In private international law we have a body of principles, varying from one jurisdiction to another but with a common core, designed to secure the protection of vested rights beyond the jurisdiction in which they were created; it furnishes such protection, in varying degrees, for rights of status, rights of property, and rights of contract. It represents a far-flung though unorganised system of mutual aid by means of faith and credit, though not 'full faith and credit', for each other's laws. Mutual aid among judicial systems tends to call for a more organised pattern. The enforcement of foreign judgments, the execution of foreign arbitral awards, the taking of evidence by letters rogatory and other forms of judicial assistance are not impossible on the basis of custom and courtesy but are increasingly governed by international agreements. Their corollaries in the criminal law, extradition and the return of fugitive offenders, are now unusual in the absence of reciprocal agreements.

In all these fields the extent and effectiveness of mutual aid is limited by the extent to which the states concerned share certain common values. No court enforces a foreign law which is contrary to the public policy of the forum; judicial assistance in all its forms is limited by public policy and generally by a requirement of reciprocity; extradition is granted only where the offence charged constitutes a crime by the law of both countries and subject to appropriate safeguards for fair trial.

The progress of mutual aid in these fields therefore depends on an increasing acceptance and consciousness of common values. The unification of private law and conclusion of general conventions on the enforcement of foreign judgments, extradition, and such matters, have been pursued hitherto on a limited geographical basis, chiefly, though not only, in Western Europe. Regional approaches to these matters are not unnatural and may be expected to remain important, but a much larger task lies ahead. With the rarest exceptions, men of all countries now travel, trade, marry, have issue and die virtually everywhere; world commerce knows neither national or regional frontiers; a fugitive offender may escape rapidly to, and seek refuge in, any part of the world. Under such conditions mutual aid by states in the enforcement of each other's laws can be only partially effective until it becomes universal in scope; but such universality presupposes an intensive world-wide effort to attain a reasonable comparability, though not necessarily uniformity, in the substantive law, and such universality can be attained without prejudice to justice and freedom only when the values and procedural safeguards embodied in the Universal Declaration of Human Rights and the United Nations Covenant on Civil and Political Rights are generally accepted.

Colossal as this task may be, the mutual aid of states in the enforcement of each other's laws is one of the foundations of international society; we can trace it back to the first beginnings of such a society, and without it the coexistence of independent states in a world community would be inconceivable.

Mutual aid in the enforcement of international decisions is in a much earlier stage of development. The principle was embodied in the Covenant of the League of Nations, which gave the Council of the League a general power to propose what measures should be taken to give effect to international judicial decisions and arbitral awards. It reappears in the Charter of the United Nations as regards both the political decisions of the Security Council and the judicial decisions of the International Court. Decisions taken by the Security Council in the discharge of its responsibility for the maintenance of international peace and security are binding upon all members of the United Nations, and the Security Council is also responsible for deciding what measures should be taken to give effect to the decisions of the International Court. We have, therefore, in respect of mutual aid in the enforcement of international decisions, a clearer principle more authoritatively proclaimed than has ever existed in respect of the mutual aid of states in the enforcement of each other's laws.

While the principle is unequivocal, the arrangements for its application are much less satisfactory. Action by the Security Council is liable to be paralysed by the difficulty of securing the necessary majority and the possibility of a veto; the practical modalities of mutual aid in the enforcement of international decisions against states present far greater difficulty than those of the enforcement of foreign laws and decisions upon individuals, and there is far less solid body of established practice for our guidance than exists in respect of mutual aid by states for the enforcement of each other's laws. The problem of methods of securing compliance with international decisions and awards is one of the crucial problems of contemporary international society. Unless we can resolve it, neither the United Nations nor the International Court of Justice can fulfil the expectations of their founders.

The problem cannot be resolved by any simple or uniform formula. As I have endeavoured to show elsewhere, different approaches may be necessary to secure compliance with different types of international decision.[1] In some cases, direct action by the Security Council calling upon members of the United Nations to take appropriate measures of

---

[1] *The Prospects of International Adjudication*, 1964, pp. 663–726.

enforcement may be possible and appropriate. In other cases, action through regional organisations or through specialised agencies in a position to exercise particular forms of pressure may be more likely to produce useful results. In some cases, it may be possible to call in aid the law enforcement machinery of particular states. There is, however, a common principle underlying all of the possible methods of securing compliance, and the principle is once more that of mutual aid. We cannot begin to spell out the principle in effective procedural arrangements until our unequivocal acceptance of the principle itself has been transformed from a juridical abstraction into a political reality. When, but only when, we pass from the stage of lip-service to the principle to that of real belief in and acceptance of it as the basis of policy will the problem of the execution of international decisions become soluble.

MUTUAL AID FOR ECONOMIC STABILITY AND GROWTH

It is in the economic field that the principle of mutual aid has attracted the widest attention in recent years. The principle has been recognised intermittently for generations; a memorable illustration of it was the British grant of 1834 in aid of the emancipation of the West Indian slaves; but only since the Second World War has it held a central place in international policy. If, indeed, it had represented a consistent philosophy and not merely an occasional interlude during the inter-war period, the great depression and the Second World War itself might perhaps have been avoided. Only if it becomes a consistent philosophy, vigorously applied in practice, can we hope to resolve the North-South tensions by comparison with which the East-West tensions of the last two decades may prove to have been an episode rather than a watershed of history.

It was in the field of monetary policy that the principle of mutual aid for economic stability and growth first crystallised into firm international obligations comprehensive in their nature and geographical extent. The International Monetary Fund is essentially a device for mutual aid in the maintenance of currency stability; the ground rules of monetary policy accepted by its members are conditions of the availability of such aid. As a plan for the relaxation of currency restrictions and the pooling of monetary reserves the Fund has been supplemented by such regional and temporary arrangements as the European Payments Union and such longer-term measures as the 'Paris club', a scheme of drawing rights whereby the leading currencies mutually support each other against strain; nor has it completely superseded the Bank for International Settlements as an instrument of cooperation among central banks. The technicalities of these experiments in monetary cooperation differ substantially and need not now detain us; they all, in varying ways and degrees, translate the principle of mutual aid in monetary matters into clear-cut international obligations.

The scope of mutual aid for economic stability and growth has now become much wider. Mutual aid for reconstruction and development on an impressive and world-wide scale has become the most distinctive new note of international policy in our time. Overseas development and welfare schemes, lend-lease and the wartime mutual aid which grew out of it, post-war relief and rehabilitation operations, the creation in 1944 of the World Bank, the Marshall Plan and European recovery programme, President Truman's Point Four, the United Nations Expanded Programme of Technical Assistance for Economic Development, the Colombo Plan, the rapid growth of bilateral programmes, the establishment of the United Nations Special Fund, the Inter-American Development Bank and the Alliance for Progress, the reorganisation of the Organisation for European Economic Cooperation into the Organisation for Economic Cooperation and Development, and the African and Asian Development Banks; all of these mark important stages in the widening acceptance of the principle proclaimed by the International Labour Organisation in the Declaration of Philadelphia that poverty anywhere is a danger to prosperity everywhere.

The general principle has found a threefold institutional expression: the complex of lending institutions developed by the World Bank, which includes the International Finance Corporation as a source of capital for private enterprise and the International Development Association as a source of easy repayment facility grants; the United Nations Development Programme, comprising the Expanded Programme of Technical Assistance and the United Nations Special Fund, now merged under unified arrangements; and the regional arrangements developed and in process of further development in Europe, the Colombo Plan area, Latin America and Africa.

In each of these institutional contexts we now have a substantial body of law governing the modalities of mutual aid, but it is the modalities rather than the broadest principles which have proved susceptible of formulation in legal terms and which it has proved necessary to formulate in such terms at this stage. The future of the whole venture is still far from fully assured and may depend in a considerable degree on the extent to which it proves possible to emphasise and crystallise the element of mutuality which is involved. If developed countries administer aid programmes as a charity or a bribe and developing countries claim them as a natural right, a substitute rather than an incentive for national effort, there will be no sufficiently solid basis for the continuity and increased scale of action which is required to meet the needs. The time may have come for an attempt to deduce from the innumerable rules and agreements governing mutual aid for economic stability and growth a body of broad principles which could gradually harden into law; the time may soon come when the formulation of such a body of principles is indispensable to the community of purpose which the whole venture presupposes. In such a body of principles the obligation to aid, and the obligation to use aid wisely, for commonly agreed purposes which represent the interest of the world community as a whole, will necessarily be complementary to each other.

Mutual aid for economic development may take the form of collective action by a number of states financed in part from external sources. The archetype of such mutual aid is the European Recovery Programme organised to administer the Marshall Plan. A striking recent illustration of it is afforded by the Indus Waters Treaty[1], which provides for Indo-Pakistani cooperation in the sharing and development of the waters of the Indus Basin and for the construction as a means of facilitating such cooperation of extensive hydraulic, irrigation and drainage works financed in part by the International Bank. The treaty proclaims the common interest of the two parties in the optimum development of the rivers of the Indus system, records their common intention to operate storage dams, barrages and irrigation canals in such a way as to avoid, as far as possible, material damage to each other, and embodies arrangements for mutual aid in respect of such matters as flood control, the avoidance of pollution and the return to its natural channels of water withdrawn for non-consumptive uses. The Mekong River Project, the exploratory stages of which have been financed by the United Nations Development Programme, furnishes a further example. Mutual aid of this type may have a particularly important future; it combines a stimulus to local initiative and collective action with the availability of much greater resources than can be locally provided. A wide range of new legal devices and forms may be necessary for the successful administration of such schemes.

[1] For text, see *Indian Journal of International Law*, vol. i, nos. 2 and 3, pp. 343–411.

An increasing shift of emphasis from aid to trade has been apparent in recent years. The United Nations Conference on Trade and Development of 1964 represents a historic landmark in this respect. Secretary-General U Thant has described it as 'the culmination of efforts and discussions over almost two decades, during which new political forces and ideas of international cooperation were gradually taking shape within the United Nations'. The action recommended by the Conference will greatly enlarge the role of the United Nations in the field of international trade and add to the broad concepts of negotiation and conciliation inherent in the Charter new conciliation procedures which are essential to carry out decisions whose ultimate purpose is to change the existing international division of labour. Mutual aid in large-scale re-adjustments of policy has never been envisaged in more dramatic and comprehensive terms. As the new policies in process of development crystallise, they will increasingly find expression in legal obligations.

The wind of change is now sweeping through the established machinery of international cooperation in trade matters. GATT, at one time regarded as a rich man's club, has renovated its policies to give greater weight to the problems of the developing countries and has adopted new provisions to foster the expansion of their trade and export earnings. It has restated its basic objectives for this purpose; has initiated steps for the reduction and elimination, as rapidly as possible, of tariffs and other barriers to imports from developing countries; has sponsored a series of cooperative undertakings to stimulate the export potential of developing countries; and has established a Trade and Development Committee as a focal point for this new work. The General Agreement on Tariffs and Trade already constitutes a body of accepted common obligations, which have now been revised to give expression to broader and more dynamic objectives.

Mutual aid in trade matters is no less necessary and important in the mutual relations of highly developed countries than in their relations with the developing world. A significant illustration of its constantly increasing scope is afforded by the arrangement recently made by the United States, thirteen European maritime nations and Japan to furnish each other through the Organisation for Economic Cooperation and Development with confidential information concerning maritime freight rates; this arrangement represents an agreed cooperative solution of a long-standing dispute between the United States and the other leading maritime carriers which had assumed a grave and acute character.

MUTUAL AID FOR SCIENTIFIC AND TECHNOLOGICAL PROGRESS

The progress of advanced science and technology has called for new applications of the principle of mutual aid in international law. The world is now a community for scientific and technological progress; even the largest States require each other's cooperation to make their programmes fully effective, to reduce the financial burden which they involve, to minimize mutual interference liable to frustrate each other's experiments and operations, to offset the danger of military surprise, and to avoid the wastage or contamination of scarce or unique resources or a common environment; all but the largest states can play an effective part in expanding the frontiers of such progress, and can share in the enjoyment of the new opportunities which it offers, only by pooling their efforts and resources for the purpose.

A wealth of illustration of the range and importance of these new applications of the principle of mutual aid is already available in the law of space; nuclear law affords similar illustrations; supersonic flight will involve further development of the manner in which the principle is already applied to aviation and telecommunications; the exploration of the ocean depths and experiments in weather control may well call for other new applications of the general principle. Nor is the significance of the principle in the scientific and technological field in any way limited to these, the most advanced frontiers of development. Flood control, hydro-electric development, erosion prevention and arid zone redevelopment are problems which frequently transcend frontiers and can, when the interests of more than one state are directly affected, be resolved only by measures of international cooperation involving an element of legal regulation based essentially on the principle of mutual aid. As the resourcefulness of scientists finds expression in new developments and possibilities as yet unforeseen, there will be a continuing challenge to the resourcefulness of statesmen, administrators and lawyers to devise methods of controlling these developments for the common good on the basis of the same principle.

For more specific illustrations let us turn to the law of space. The Declaration of Legal Principles Governing the Activities of States in the Exploration and Use of Outer Space, adopted by the General Assembly of the United Nations on 13 December 1963[1], and the Treaty on Principles Governing the Activities of States in the Exploration and Use of Outer Space, including the Moon and Other Celestial Bodies, provide that 'the exploration and use of outer space shall be carried on for the

[1] General Assembly Resolution 1962 (XVIII).

benefit and in the interests of all mankind' and that 'in the exploration and use of outer space, states shall be guided by the principle of cooperation and mutual assistance and shall conduct all their activities in outer space with due regard for the corresponding interests of other states'. They also give a more specific content to this general principle of mutual aid in three particular contexts. They require mutual consultation concerning potentially harmful space activities or experiments; they provide for the return to the state of registry of objects launched into outer space and their component parts found beyond the limits of the state of registry on their return to earth; and they specify that states shall regard astronauts as envoys of mankind in outer space, and shall render to them all possible assistance, and facilitate their safe and prompt return, in the event of accident, distress or emergency landing on the territory of a foreign state or on the high seas. The principle is now being spelled out in greater detail by the negotiation of an international agreement concerning repatriation and return. It is already applied in the field of space telecommunications by the International Telecommunication Regulations and in that of meteorology by the arrangements for the sharing of information from meteorological satellites made by the World Meteorological Organisation. It has found expression in an increasing number of common ventures, ranging from the United Nations sponsored international equatorial rocket-launching facility at Thumba in South India (soon to be followed by a similar facility at Natal in Brazil) and the potentially world-wide Global Communications Satellite System, through such regional undertakings as the European Space Research Organisation and the European Launcher Development Organisation and such joint ventures of the leading space powers as the U.S.A.-U.S.S.R. joint geodetic, meteorological, Echo-relay and space biology programmes, to the arrangements with other states made by each of the space powers for supporting services for its own programme. In all these arrangements, mutual aid in execution is accompanied by provision for the common enjoyment of the benefits secured.

The concept for mutual aid for scientific and technological progress opens up vistas without precedent or parallel in history. The legal framework of such mutual aid may be expected to be a major branch of international law within a generation.

CONSULTATION AND CONSENSUS

Let us assume a general desire to apply the principle of mutual aid over an ever-widening range of common interests. How can we give it institutional form and practical effectiveness? We must do so primarily by devising for each type of case institutional arrangements appropriate to the needs of the case. There may be common patterns for certain types of case, but they will nearly always require adaptation to the needs of the particular case. The crucial problems will, however, generally arise in the process of evolving such arrangements. How far are there general considerations of policy by which we should be guided in our desire to make of the principle of mutual aid a practical reality? Two such considerations are of special importance at the present juncture; others may be of equal importance at some later stage.

In the first place, the freedom of action of states is increasingly abridged by widespread obligations of consultation. Such consultation is now recognised good practice over a wide range of political matters, within alignments, as between alignments, and among non-aligned countries; the further development of such consultation can play a substantial part in promoting the sense of community and relaxing tensions. As opportunity offers there may be great advantage in developing recognised good practice into accepted legal obligation; this is clearly in process of happening in respect of emergency action for collective or individual self-defence or on humanitarian grounds.

The principle of consultation is as fundamental to contemporary international economic policy as is the renunciation of force to the law governing the settlement of international disputes; it is the central concept of the International Monetary Fund and the General Agreement on Tariffs and Trade; in the Organisation for Economic Cooperation and Development and such more intimate economic associations as the European Economic Community, the European Free Trade Association and the similar arrangements being developed in other continents it plays a leading role; the United Nations Conference on Trade and Development has greatly expanded the range of its probable further applications; in all these contexts the policy of consultation concerning economic and financial matters of mutual concern is increasingly maturing into accepted legal obligations any underestimate of which is certain to provoke a sharp reaction and liable to be the occasion of measures of retortion against the action taken without consultation. Full consultation is likewise the basis of mutual aid in the field of science and technology. The United Nations Scientific Conferences on the Peaceful Uses of Atomic Energy and the Application of Science and Technology to Economic Development have been an important stimulus to such consultation, which they have made politically respectable by the relaxation of security restrictions; the similar conference on the Peaceful Uses of Outer Space now projected may be expected to supplement the work of the Committee on Space Research of the International Council of Scientific Unions in the same manner. The habit of consultation thus engendered may also be expected to be transformed into legal obligations as circumstances require; this stage has already been reached in the case of potentially harmful space activities or experiments in respect of which mutual consultation is now required by the Declaration of Legal Principles Governing the Activities of States in the Exploration and Use of Outer Space and the Treaty on Principles Governing the Activities of States in the Exploration and Use of Outer Space, including the Moon and Other Celestial Bodies. The recognition of a similar obligation in respect of other experiments or schemes which may affect significantly the natural environment of more than one state is highly desirable.[1]

Secondly, mutual aid presupposes as its basis a consensus. It cannot be created or maintained by a majority decision of those to be aided. This has become particularly apparent, and is now generally if reluctantly accepted, in the economic field. A group of seventy-five developing countries may be an invaluable instrument of negotiation with developed countries, greatly reducing disparity in bargaining power; it is not a basis for decision-making by a majority which excludes essential parties to the decision to be taken. In the scientific and technological field the principle also commands wide acceptance; the Agreement establishing Interim Arrangements for a Global Communications Satellite System, for instance, specifically embodies it; it is increasingly recognised to have an important bearing on the satisfactory financing of international organisations, and in particular of large-scale aid and development programmes. In matters of security and law enforcement the consensus required must necessarily fall short of that of the law-breaker or defaulter upon an obligation; but only on the basis of a wide consensus can international peace and security be maintained, or international decisions enforced, without precipitating conflicts as dangerous as those which it is sought to resolve. This was the *rationale* of the veto in the Security Council, however unsatisfactory it may have proved in practice. The substitution of the principle of majority decision for that of unanimity as the basis of the functioning of international organisations marked a decisive stage in their development; no sane person would now

---

[1] *Cf.* C. W. Jenks, *Law, Freedom and Welfare*, 1963, pp. 33–49 and 'Liability for Ultra-hazardous Activities in International Law', *Recueil des Cours de l'Académie de Droit International*, vol. 117, 1966 (I), pp. 101–198.

wish to revert to the old order; but we have not yet learned how to operate the new order wisely. Majorities in international organisations are unlike those in national democratic processes in that the basis of calculation is inevitably an artificial one. When a nation of 600 million and a nation of a quarter of a million have the same voting power it becomes necessary to weigh votes rather than to count them. Whether one likes it or not, the significance in the world of the U.S.A. or the U.S.S.R. cannot be measured by that of the Maldive Islands. We must, therefore, if we seek reality in international organisation, evolve ways of ensuring that important decisions represent a consensus embracing the weight of power and influence necessary to make them effective; in this matter, China, India and Japan have the same interest as the U.S.A., the U.S.S.R., Britain, France and Germany. But this interest is not limited to the great powers of today or tomorrow; it is an interest of the community as a whole. We cannot have effectiveness in international organisation unless decisions reflect the power to make them effective, and without such effectiveness we have a mere façade unable to protect the weak, to restrain the strong, or to mobilise affluence in the war against want.

The progress of man from mutual aid in the village community to mutual aid in space defines the dimensions in which the contemporary international lawyer must envisage his task and opportunity. We are wrestling with problems of a wholly new magnitude and complexity. We cannot hope to resolve them with the intellectual equipment of yester-year. We must approach them with an acute sense of their interdependence upon each other. We cannot apply one set of values to mutual aid for economic stability and growth and mutual aid for scientific and technological progress and a wholly different and less responsible set of values to mutual aid for the maintenance of peace and security and mutual aid for law enforcement. Let us therefore see the picture as a whole and so develop the principle of mutual aid in international law that the law becomes an effective bulwark of the peace, freedom and welfare of all mankind.

7

Tolerance and good-neighbourliness as concepts of international law[1]

The peoples of the United Nations have proclaimed in the Charter their common determination 'to practice tolerance and live together in peace with one another as good neighbours'. By affirming in this solemn manner the interdependence of peace, tolerance and good neighbourliness they have introduced a new scale of values into the assessment of the legal obligations implicit in civilised conduct, a new scale of values no less important than the renunciation of armed force save in the common interest, the principle of uniting their strength to maintain international peace and security, the reaffirmation of faith in fundamental human rights, and the promotion of social progress and better standards of life in larger freedom. The impact on the law of these other aims set forth in the Preamble to the Charter has been widely canvassed in the extensive literature relating to the renunciation of force, collective security, human rights and international economic and social cooperation, but the extent to which the concepts of tolerance and good neighbourliness may have any tangible legal content has been little discussed.

Here in Singapore, where the Malay, Hindu, Buddhist and Islamic cultures have interacted for centuries with those of the West and of China, it is particularly apposite to stress the contemporary importance of transforming the seminal ideas of tolerance and good neighbourliness from moral precepts into legal concepts and political realities. South-East Asia may be the decisive arena in which the nations learn to practice tolerance and live together with each other as good neighbours or destroy their common heritage of unbounded opportunity. It is, with the Eastern Mediterranean, one of the areas where, without a full measure of tolerance and good neighbourliness, intractable local problems are both insoluble as such and liable to precipitate wider dangers, but it is also the arena where a drama on an altogether bigger scale is unfolding. It

[1] An address to the Faculty of Law and Extramural Department of the University of Singapore, 5 December 1966.

will inevitably be one of the areas where the western and oriental traditions come, or fail to come, to terms with each other in evolving a new
synthesis of political ethics and legal principle to guide their future
conduct, adjust their conflicting interests and harmonise their mutual
relations.

   To evolve a synthesis satisfactory for this purpose we must extend our
horizon beyond a limited group of legal systems such as the civil law and
common law systems, and widen our field of vision to include the varied
legal cultures of all mankind. The concept that any one culture has a
monopoly of legal wisdom is no less an anachronism than the concept
that any one culture is the centre of the universe. The process involved
is similar to that which has been made familiar to you by the legal history
of Malaya, where the 'ādat law, Islamic law and the common law have all
contributed to the synthesis represented by the contemporary law.[1]

   In this process we must expect the characteristic features of Chinese
and Japanese jurisprudence to be important factors. How permanent an
influence these features will prove to be in a rapidly changing orient is
inevitably a somewhat speculative matter, but some of them may well
outlive the most far-reaching political, economic and social changes.
Among these are jurisprudential concepts closely related to the ideas of
tolerance and good neighbourliness.

   The classical jurisprudence of China rests upon the fundamental
principles of *tao* and *li* and a preference for conciliation rather than
adjudication as a means of settling disputes. By *tao* is meant the creative
principle of natural order and harmony. By *li* is meant an ethical and
ritual obligation to observe standards of good conduct which express an
ideal of social harmony emphasizing the obligation of the individual to
society. Conciliation is a method of adjusting disputes in the light of
these principles rather than of enforcing rights. All these concepts have
a bearing on the clothing in legal form of the political aims and moral
precepts set forth in the Preamble to the Charter. *Tao*, the creative
principle of natural order and harmony, implies both tolerance and good
neighbourliness. *Li*, the ethical equivalent of legal obligation, likewise
involves both tolerance and good neighbourliness. The Japanese concept
of *giri*, a composite of obligations to the world and obligations to one's
own name, includes both elements of tolerance and good neighbourliness
and elements hardly compatible therewith.[2] Conciliation, which has

---

[1] *Cf.* S. Gordon, *ed., Malay 'Ādat and Islām*, Singapore, 1966.
[2] Yosiyuki Noda, *Introduction au Droit japonais*, Librairie Dalloz, Paris, 1966,
pp. 191–200.

always been a characteristic feature of both Chinese[1] and Japanese[2] law, may be regarded as a procedural expression of the ideas of tolerance and good neighbourliness. It is a useful device for clarifying to the parties their factual and legal positions, but it is inept to enforce rights against power and authority or to reconcile the recalcitrant to social change, and is as defective in this respect internationally as on the national plane.

The '*ādat* law of Malaysia and Indonesia may also contribute concepts which have a significant bearing on the relevance to the law of such seminal ideas as tolerance and good neighbourliness. '*Ādat* is more than custom or convention as understood by the common law and civil law disciplines; it regulates the entire life of the community. A common '*ādat* involves a recognised pattern of close cooperation in all the important events in the life of the individual and the community. We must not strain such concepts beyond their historical content or their present relevance. The concept of an '*ādat* handed down from generation to generation, which, in the Minangkabau saying, 'doesn't crack with the heat or rot in the rain', is ill-fitted for a world of change. The '*ādat* of a community is, moreover, local to itself, the distinctive intellectual legacy of its forefathers. Our need today is to develop from the tolerant acceptance of our neighbours' '*ādats* a common '*ādat* for mankind. But the limitations of such concepts do not impair their validity and relevance within proper limits.

In having recourse to such concepts from the traditional legal systems of Asia we must at all times be conscious that the world in which we are called upon to apply them is changing to an extent and at a rate for which history affords no precedent. New political forces, new strategic problems, new economic and social aspirations, new cultural attitudes, new scientific and technological possibilities have completely transformed the outlook and preoccupations of human society. How much further change upon the scale to which we have now become accustomed will proceed we cannot hope to foresee. We must be content to grope, and at times to gamble, knowing that the whole future of man may depend on how enlightened a boldness we bring to the task. The law cannot remain immutable in a universe of change. We need a new approach to the problem of giving an effective practical expression in the law to such concepts as tolerance and good neighbourliness, an approach

[1] T'ang-Tsu Ch'ii, *Law and Society in Traditional China*, Mouton and Co., The Hague, 1961, pp. 226–79; S. van der Sprenkel, *Legal Institutions in Manchu China*, Athlone Press, London, edn. 1966, pp. 112–23.

[2] Dan Fenno Henderson, *Conciliation and Japanese Law*, University of Washington Press, Seattle, 1965, 2 vols.

which has been well defined in a valuable and fascinating work, by the Attorney-General of Singapore:

> The Muslims of today should treat the circumstances of today as the great jurists did theirs and try to face their special problems in the light of the public good, as they did. . . . It is altogether unrealistic to seek from the jurists of the past solutions to the problems of our own age—an age of which they could have no knowledge. . . . While the unequivocal ordinances of the Holy *Qur'ān* and the *Sunnah* must for all times remain valid as the unchangeable Muslim law, the Muslims are not only permitted but definitely encouraged to develop side by side with this unchanging law, a changeable and changing law, which would apply the spirit and the actual injunctions of the Divine Law to the social requirements of each time and place.[1]

Much the same may be said of the law of nations. In the law of nations the concepts of tolerance and good neighbourliness belong to the unchanging law, but their practical applications to the changeable and changing law.

We must increasingly expect the process of giving legal expression to new social needs and sociological trends to reflect the prevailing temper of developing societies. Law, as a contemporary Indonesian scholar has said, is not just the outgrowth of a developing society:

> Its role in guiding and stimulating a society's growth in a desired direction is no less important. Law is the twin of education; each helps the other to shape the new society and its culture. And it is particularly those nations lagging behind in the technological advances of this modern age that cannot avoid the necessity of making responsible use of this second function of law.[2]

We may expect, and should encourage, the developing societies, whose role in determining the future authority and influence of law in world affairs is now decisive,[3] to be insistent in urging such a responsible use of the corresponding function of the law of nations.

Such an approach will inevitably pose some difficult dilemmas for some of the traditional schools of legal thought. Such schools of thought still have a powerful grip on the legal mind in both the most and the least advanced of contemporary societies; they are equally prevalent in the

---

[1] A. Ibrahim, *Islāmic Law in Malaya*, Singapore, 1965, p. 117.

[2] S. T. Alisjahbana, *Indonesia: Social and Cultural Revolution*, Oxford University Press, Kuala Lumpur, 1966, pp. 76–7.

[3] *Cf.* Jenks, *The Common Law of Mankind*, 1958.

most liberal and the most regimented of cultures. In wrestling with these dilemmas we must be guided by the essential newness of the political, economic, cultural and technological context in which the law now operates. In the new context of the world of accelerated change in which we live, the oldest and most fundamental of legal principles have new and newly-important practical applications. These cannot be dismissed as 'new law' beyond the scope of the judicial process or useful juridical speculation. They are essential to the continued vitality of any law which can be developed by legal thought and administered by the judicial process. Let us therefore review in this spirit the status of tolerance and good neighbourliness in the law.

How far broad standards of conduct can be refined into measurable obligations is one of the crucial problems of every developing legal system. In the dissenting opinions delivered in the International Court of Justice in the *South West Africa Cases* by Judges Wellington Koo[1] and Tanaka[2] we have impressive examples of the judicial application of broad standards to specific facts. How far can such broad standards as tolerance and good neighbourliness be materialised into specific obligations by custom, treaty, adjudication or the practice of international organisations? We are at much too early a stage of development for any dogmatism in the matter to be wise, but there are a number of lines along which the law is at present evolving, may evolve, or should be encouraged to evolve, which appear to be worthy of fuller exploration.

Toleration as an ethical and political principle was enshrined in the heritage of common lawyers by John Locke, but there is as little mention of it in Blackstone, who includes apostasy and heresy among crimes and misdemeanours, as in Bracton or Coke. Nor do international lawyers give it any recognised place among their basic concepts. Tolerance is nevertheless the foundation of the coexistence in freedom of differing religions, races, cultures and economic and social systems. Presupposing such fundamental axioms as the unity of mankind, the equality of man, the relativity of truth and the mutability of destiny and circumstance, it represents the indispensable social and political foundation without which no world community is practicable and no international legal order conceivable. It was the basis on which Christianity and Islam renounced the Crusades and the *jihad*, on which Europe rebuilt a common polity after the Wars of Religion and again after the French Revolution, on which Western Europe reaffirmed after the Second World War the unity of its common civilisation, and on which the

---

[1] 1966, I.C.J. 232–8.   [2] *Ibid.*, 278–316.

British Commonwealth in its pre-1947 form evolved into the present multiracial Commonwealth. It is the basis on which the Cold War in Europe is being terminated. It is the only basis on which the peace of Asia can be restored and assured.

Tolerance implies a long view of the probable future development of apparently irreconcilable philosophies and interests. There is ample historical justification for taking such a long view. The Muslim attitude to the law of nations, originally based on the theory of a universal state, has accommodated itself to the membership in the United Nations of twenty-one Muslim states.[1] The communist attitude to the law of nations, originally based on a theory of universal revolution and a system of Soviets transcending national boundaries, has accommodated itself to the membership in the United Nations of ten communist states variously related to each other.[2] The Chinese attitude to the law of nations, originating with the concept of China as the Celestial Empire, accommodated itself to membership of the League of Nations and participation in the creation of United Nations.[3] Neither the *jihad* nor the Communist Manifesto of 1848 can be reconciled with the Charter of the United Nations, but this has not precluded the development of new forms and traditions of international collaboration wholly unforeseeable by Mahomet or Karl Marx. We cannot assume that this process of evolution has reached its term.

The critical dilemma of tolerance has always been how far to preserve it against the intolerant. Tolerance of intolerance may culminate in the violent suppression of tolerance; the curbing of intolerance may culminate in tolerance being untrue to itself. There is no fully satisfactory answer to what is essentially a question of good judgment. The Universal Declaration of Human Rights and United Nations Covenants of Human Rights recognise the dilemma by specifying that nothing therein 'may be interpreted as implying for any state, group of persons or person any right to engage in any activity or to perform any act aimed at the destruction of any of the rights or freedoms' recognised therein. How far can these general considerations of policy be materialised into specific obligations? In some respects, it is submitted, they can.

[1] Majid Khadduri, *War and Peace in the Law of Islam*, Johns Hopkins: Oxford U.P., 1955.

[2] See, for instance, J. N. Hazard, 'Soviet Law' in *Sovereignty Within the Law*, Larson, Jenks *et al.*, 1965, pp. 286–98, and K. Grzybowski, *The Socialist Commonwealth of Nations: Organisation and Institutions*, Yale U.P., 1964.

[3] L. Tung, *China and Some Phases of International Law*, Oxford U.P., New York, 1940.

Tolerance accepts diversity. The obligation of tolerance implicit in civilised conduct by virtue of the Charter therefore includes the obligation to accept diversity. The obligation is equally binding on both sides to an ideological conflict. It includes the obligation not to withhold recognition or debar participation in the United Nations on ideological grounds. It includes the obligation to refrain from subversion or aggression alleged to be justified on ideological grounds. These obligations are more than counsels of morality or political expediency. They are the reflection in specific legal obligations of the determination to practice tolerance proclaimed by the Charter. They are necessary and complementary elements in any lasting settlement of the affairs of South-East Asia, the region which at present suffers most from the fact that the United Nations is not yet universal in effective membership and influence.

Tolerance precludes discrimination on political, racial or religious grounds. The Declaration of Philadelphia of 1944, now an integral part of the Constitution of the International Labour Organisation, the Universal Declaration of Human Rights of 1948, and the United Nations Covenants of Human Rights of 1966 enunciate the general principle that the elimination of such discrimination is a major objective of international effort. The obligation to refrain from such discrimination is increasingly finding expression in firm international obligations, typified by the I.L.O. Discrimination (Employment and Occupation) Convention, 1958, as of 1 August 1967 ratified by 60 States, the Unesco Convention against Discrimination in Education of 1960, and the United Nations Convention on the Elimination of All Forms of Racial Discrimination of 1965. These declarations and conventions have a significance in the development of international law comparable to that of the Declaration of the Rights of Man and the Citizen in the history of civil liberties. A common respect for our common humanity is passing from the realm of philosophical acceptance to that of legal obligation, formulated in international agreements and national laws and regulations and enforced where need be by appropriate procedures. The principle is of major importance for the future peace of South-East Asia, today as for centuries one of the most racially heterogeneous areas of the world.

Tolerance presupposes freedom of information and restraint from defamation. The law concerning information and defamation is at very different stages of development. The principle of freedom of information, though much discussed at United Nations Conferences on the subject, has not yet found expression in any generally accepted legal obligations. The practical elements in the problem include: freedom to seek information at its source from unreasonable restriction by either the country whose scholars, news media or public are in search of the information or the country where the information is sought; positive steps to facilitate the freer flow of news and other information, scientific knowledge and data, and cultural materials across political and ideological curtains and other boundaries; freedom from censorship, on any but reasonably interpreted security grounds, of incoming or outgoing news, periodicals and books; freedom from jamming of international broadcasts; and other similar matters. Action in respect of these matters involves changes in national policies concerning freedom of access to uncontrolled information, more liberal passport and visa policies, and comprehensive cultural exchange agreements and arrangements. These are large and controversial questions of policy involving in an acute degree the problem of how to secure an effective reciprocity; progress concerning them would involve important changes of attitude on all sides and in particular on the part of those whose policies on these matters are least liberal. It does not, however, follow that the formulation of appropriate standards in regard to them in legal instruments cannot play a significant part in stimulating and crystallising the necessary changes of policy. Even if draft instruments in which such standards were formulated did not become immediately operative, they would constitute a continuing offer to give by reciprocal action a firm legal basis to the practice of tolerance in the things of the mind.

While freedom of information as a legal obligation requires novel concepts and procedures, not yet clearly thought through and still to be accepted in principle and tested in practice, defamation is a recognised tort, no less important in contemporary international relations than in municipal law. The obligation of tolerance implicit in civilised conduct by virtue of the terms of the Charter includes an obligation of members of the United Nations to refrain from making, authorising, or permitting the use of official media for, statements defamatory of other members, and to restrain by appropriate legal procedures other conduct within their jurisdiction which is defamatory of their fellow members. The general fulfilment of this obligation has an important bearing on the future peace of South-East Asia, now, alas, one of the leading cockpits of the ideological conflicts of our time.

Good neighbourliness, like tolerance, is a principle with a potential of applications in specific legal obligations which we have only begun to explore. Good neighbourliness begins with respect for the territory of one's neighbour, one of the most elementary of the traditional principles of international law, now specifically restated in the provision of the Charter that all states shall refrain from the threat or use of force against the territorial integrity of any state.[1] Without this principle there can be no orderly world community. Without it there can be no stable peace, in South-East Asia or elsewhere.

Good neighbourliness precludes the use of one's own territory in a manner which constitutes a danger for one's neighbours. Allowing one's territory to be used for armed attack upon one's neighbours has long been a recognised and grave violation of the law of nations. The principle of which this rule is an expression has, however, a much wider range of potential applications. Contemporary scientific and technological developments have made possible a whole series of new uses of one's territory, including outer space, the tapping of underground resources, industrial processes involving air and water pollution and nuclear activities, which may constitute a danger or detriment to neighbouring territory and its inhabitants hardly less serious in its potential consequences than armed attack. The principle of good neighbourliness implies both a general obligation of care in respect of these matters and, to an extent not yet clearly defined, responsibility without fault for the risks arising from such activities. We may expect the scope and modalities of these obligations to be more precisely defined in future proceedings before international courts and tribunals and other international bodies and by means of appropriate international agreements.[2] The prohibition upon allowing one's territory to be used for armed attack upon one's neighbours has an immediate bearing on the peace and stability of South-East Asia; the principle applicable to the conduct of ultra-hazardous activities upon one's territory has become of even wider application with the ever wider diffusion of the newest technological know-how and processes.

Good neighbourliness includes the obligation to respect the political independence and economic and social system of one's neighbour. Some elements in this obligation are well defined; others remain conjectural or imprecise. The prohibition by the Charter of the threat or use of force includes such threat or use against the political independence of any state, but leaves unanswered such questions as how much more than refraining from the threat or use of force may be involved in respecting

[1] Article 2 (4).

[2] *Cf.* Jenks, 'Liability for Ultra-hazardous Activities in International Law', in *Recueil des Cours de l'Académie de Droit international*, vol. 117, 1966 (I), pp. 101–198.

political independence, and what obligations the mutual respect for each other of divergent economic and social systems may involve in matters of economic policy. These obligations must as a minimum include a duty to refrain from measures deliberately designed to disrupt the rival system; more positively construed they may include a duty not to discriminate in economic matters against the rival system and not to debar it from the fullest participation which the differences of system allow in mutually profitable economic intercourse. The further elaboration of this approach into a body of mutually accepted obligations may have an important bearing on the future peace and stability of South-East Asia.

Good neighbourliness finds fuller expression in mutual aid. The general concept of mutual aid has many applications in contemporary international law. They include mutual aid for the maintenance of peace and security, mutual aid in law enforcement, mutual aid for economic stability and growth, and mutual aid for scientific and technological progress. In respect of all of these matters the principle has already been extensively translated into specific international obligations, but there remains great scope for giving it, through the Asian Development Bank, the Mekong River Project, and a wide range of possible similar schemes, a more precise application in matters vitally affecting the welfare and progress of South-East Asia.

Tolerance and good neighbourliness are more than moral precepts or political slogans; they are seminal concepts which are a potential source of specific legal obligations. They have a recognised status in the law by reason of the Preamble to the Charter of the United Nations; they reflect the principles of *tao* and *li* which were the accepted basis of traditional Chinese law and therefore represent an appropriate framework for a renewed dialogue between western and oriental cultures; they are central to the role of law as the twin of education in developing societies; their potential implications have a direct bearing on many of the immediate problems of South-East Asia. A comprehensive and imaginative study of tolerance and good neighbourliness as concepts of international law would be a timely contribution to the revitalisation of international law in response to the needs of our time.

There is great need for a solid study of the subject undertaken with scholarly detachment, but it is vital to see the question in the large. Let us, as men have done since *The Book of Changes*, look forward to the day when the Age of Disorder gives way to the Age of Complete Peace-and-Equality. There can be no Age of Complete Peace-and-Equality without tolerance and good neighbourliness. Tolerance and good neighbourliness cannot be reconciled with the concept that any nation is 'The Central Nation'. They presuppose the no less seminal principle of the equality of all mankind. As the most cosmopolitan and utopian in outlook of Chinese political philosophers, K'ang Yu-Wei, has said 'The coming to birth of all men proceeds from Heaven. All are brothers. All are truly equal.'[1] We find in Islam the same principle expressed in the saying of the Prophet: 'People are all equal as the teeth of a comb.'[2] The principle is immanent in Buddhism. It is the essence of Christianity.

Within the universal community of mankind the rights of each rest upon the rights of all and the status and dignity of each nation rests upon a common respect, founded in tolerance and practised in good neighbourliness, for the status and dignity of all nations. To make these principles effective as the foundation of policy we must give them a recognised place and content in the common law of mankind. We must do so by the recognised methods of the law and within the acknowledged limits of legal technique, but we must not become the slaves of the technicalities which we have evolved to serve us. Legal methods and technique must be the tool of these high purposes and not the masters of our souls.

Tolerance and good neighbourliness are attributes of freedom. In freedom alone can they flourish. Of freedom they are both the fruit and the seed. Condoning no departure from the high standards which they postulate, they are the vital principle without which those standards cannot maintain themselves. They are the basis of law, the hallmark of freedom, an essential element in welfare. Let us, therefore, as free men practice tolerance, living in peace with each other as good neighbours under a common law of mankind founded in the Charter of the United Nations, and let us bring to the current problems of the law the creative imagination without which our professional skill will be unequal to this larger density.

[1] K'ang Yu-Wei, *Ta T'ung Shu, The One-World Philosophy of K'ang Yu-Wei*, trans. L. Thompson, Allen & Unwin, 1958.

[2] *Cf*. Sayed Kotb, *Social Justice in Islam*, American Council of Learned Societies, Washington D.C., 1953, pp. 45–55.

8

Freedom under law in the world community[1]

'A new birth of freedom' is the greatest hope of our time. Within our lifetimes the principle of authority which has underpinned human society since man first walked the earth has been called in question everywhere. It no longer dominates the family, the local community, industrial life, the nation or the world society. Rank and status no longer create any expectation of humble deference; age and sex no longer inspire respectful obedience; religion can no longer rely on an instinctive acceptance of its dogma and precepts; and what has happened in the social relations of men and women and in the attitude of the citizen towards church and state is now happening in the relations of states towards each other. The contemporary evolution of international society, as of social life generally, presents indeed a curious paradox. The traditional power structures inherited from the past, and the measure of equilibrium based upon them, are dissolving everywhere. Within the state their place has been taken in large measure by the authority of the state itself; this has been both an inspiring and a disconcerting development, inspiring because of the opportunities which it offers for a sustained vigour of action in political, economic and social advance unthinkable to earlier generations, disconcerting not only as a potential challenge to the freedom and dignity of the individual but also because of the dangers which it presents, and may sometimes conceal, of the inherent vitality of society being thinned and congealed by the authority and discipline of the state as such or of some barren or destructive ideology which controls a particular state. In the world community no comparable focus of authority has yet evolved, but the United Nations represents an attempt, on the success of which the whole future of man depends, to provide the nucleus for a similar development which will inevitably pose a similar dilemma. Secretary-General U

[1] An address to the Faculty of Law of the Imperial University of Tokyo, 19 January 1965.

Thant has said that the greatest problem of our time is 'to make the world safe for diversity'. That is the essential task of international law today. How is the task to be fulfilled?

We can hope to achieve it only if we have a clear and strong sense of our purpose as being to secure freedom under law in a dynamic, but nevertheless reasonably stable, world community. Let us then examine briefly together each of the major elements in this approach—

freedom as the purpose and justification of law;

law as the bulwark and compass of freedom;

the perpetual antinomy of stability and change; and

the universality of concern and perspective implied in the concept of a world community.

Let us first consider freedom as the purpose and justification of law. Law is never its own justification. Only in the slave state is it the badge and measure of its own authority. It is the framework of disciplined restraint without which order becomes tyranny and freedom anarchy. But there is a fundamental difference between the relationship of law to order and the relationship of law to freedom. Order, like law, is a means; freedom is an end. 'Good order is the first of all good things' only because without it things more intrinsically good are unattainable. Freedom is the true end of man; it becomes an evil only when so exercised as to destroy its own true self.

Some will of course object that law and freedom, while necessary qualifications to each other, are nevertheless antithetical to each other, and that the true end of law is justice rather than freedom. But justice is not a self-defining concept and there is a profound sense in which freedom, as a moral opportunity rather than an absence of restraint, is the essence and measure of justice.

Let us assume, then, that the vocation of the law, of all law, is freedom. In what sense is freedom the vocation of international law? Whose freedom is it the function of international law to promote? It cannot be the freedom of the state. It cannot be the freedom of any occupational group or interest within or beyond the state. It must be the freedom of man. The state, and groupings based on economic interests within or beyond the state, are conveniences of social organisation; we can no longer regard them as moral entities existing in their own right; they have a valid claim to authority and freedom only in so far as they fulfil human need by promoting and ensuring the freedom of man. Let us therefore assume as our first postulate that the primary purpose of international law is to promote the freedom of man; from this it follows that the only valid basis for judging the value and effectiveness of international law is the extent to which it promotes and secures human freedom.

Freedom is, however, a social concept; the freedom of each must be reconciled with the freedom of all. Law represents the discipline without which human freedom would be perpetually at the mercy of craft and guile, power and terror. Human freedom can be a reality only within a firm framework of legal obligation. This has always been true within the national community; it is no less true on the wider stage of world affairs.

Without the proscription of violence, the principle of third-party judgment, the legal limitation of self-help, the recognised obligation of good faith, and the duty to refrain from wilful or negligent harm to one's neighbour, the concept of freedom loses all civilised content. These things are the necessary equivalent and expression in world affairs of the traditional elements of social obligation which constitute the recognised discipline of family and national life. Let us therefore assume as our second postulate that international law can fulfil its primary purpose of promoting the freedom of man only by establishing a firm framework of legal obligation which will inevitably limit, in some respects severely, the freedom of the state.

Wherein should man be free, and wherein must he accept the rule of law and the restraint of legal obligation? Wherein should the state be free, and wherein must it accept the rule of law and the restraint of legal obligation? These are formidable questions at any time. They are particularly difficult in a world of cataclysmic political, economic and social change, when the old values of yesterday have dissolved and are dissolving, and the new values of tomorrow are not yet clearly defined, still less fully accepted. In the vortex in which we live there can be no final answers, but an impassive acceptance of the relativity of all things can spell only disaster. We must find tentative answers for each successive phase of the crisis through which we are living, content if we are able at each such phase to find an answer which leaves us free to seek a further answer in the succeeding phase. We must therefore assume as our third postulate that international law can give no final answer today to the problems of tomorrow. We must reconcile ourselves to living throughout our lifetimes with the interplay of stability and change in a world which may have, and I venture to affirm has, found a reasonably clear sense of direction, but is still groping, at times ineffectually, to devise ways of achieving goals which have won general acceptance. International law can make a useful contribution to the solution of the problems of our time only if it remains boldly experimental, but nevertheless restrained, in temper and spirit.

We seek freedom; we seek it in the rule of law; we seek it in the experimental temper of our time. We can hope to find it only if we are prepared to take the world as our parish and accept the obligations which the determination to make freedom a reality for all men everywhere presupposes for ourselves. If we believe that freedom under law is the greatest hope and challenge of our time; if we believe freedom to be the end but law the necessary means; if we believe that the law, like life, progresses by experiment and error, and reaches finality only in death; if we believe that no man, and no nation, can remain an island in an age of nuclear danger and opportunity: then we must find in the negotiation of firm international understandings concerning human rights, and in the establishment of effective procedures for promoting and ensuring their application, one of the great political adventures of all time in which it is a proud privilege to participate. No nation demeans itself by being a pioneer in any phase or aspect of this great enterprise.

To achieve these objectives we need a wider consensus, within nations and among nations. Majority solutions are a necessary expedient of practical life. Without them a stagnation in the solution of both national and international problems inconceivable to the temper and tempo of the modern world is almost inevitable. Majority solutions are, nevertheless, at best a second best. The greatest value and virtue of the possibility of majority action, and the knowledge that majority action will be taken if no better result can be secured, is to induce a general reasonableness of approach, and willingness to negotiate and compromise which makes possible a wider basis of decision. But reasonableness and patience resolve problems only when they are general. The rhythm of life does not permit of missing heartbeats and, failing a general reasonableness which finds expression in mutual concessions permitting of effective action, the world, like the state, must wrestle with its problems as best it can, with poise, tolerance and humanity, but with decision. This is one of the fundamental truths of political organisation; the harmony, resilience and strength of national societies, and their capacity to adjust without undue strain to changing challenges, depend in large measure on the extent to which the acceptance of this truth becomes instinctive, and majorities and minorities alike learn to live within the pattern of mutual adjustment which the search for a wide consensus as the basis for the prosperity and progress of the community as a whole presupposes. The progress of the world community, and its success in securing freedom under law for all men everywhere, depends on the success with which it learns to combine consensus, as the basis of the widest possible range of the common decisions with which the world as a whole must live, with a vigour of action which cannot allow itself to be paralysed by failure to achieve by consensus a reasonable result within a reasonable time. In the nature of the case these considerations cannot be expressed as a legal principle; they are not even the seed-bed of a legal principle; but they define the only climate of philosophical approach and political temper within which the world community can hope to achieve a rational solution for its most vital problems on the basis of the rule of law.

Certainly this is true of all international action for the protection of human rights. No international principle or convention relating to any human right can in itself solve all of the problems of application to which it will necessarily give rise. In this there is nothing surprising. No declaration of human rights in any national constitution has ever resolved the problems which it poses. The way to progress lies in formulating or restating a guiding principle when social evolution has reached a stage at which it becomes possible to reach a sufficient consensus on the principle and then gradually working out its detailed applications. A constitutional guarantee of freedom of speech or association becomes effective through the practice and jurisprudence which spells out its implications. There would be no freedom of speech or association anywhere if it had been necessary to determine with precision the scope and limitations of such freedom when establishing the principle. Life must trust itself; a living society must trust its own vitality and its own wisdom; a living law must trust those who live by it to apply old principles to new problems with integrity and imagination.

The viability of any legal system depends on the degree of mutual confidence which exists among those whose life as a society it governs. Only by expressing and fostering mutual confidence can the law reflect and respond to the quest for justice which has been the perennial goal of legal philosophers since Prince Shotoku in the Japanese tradition[1] or Plato in the tradition of the West. Only by being so conceived, negotiated, adopted and explained as to command such confidence can new law, and especially new law on new, difficult and controversial problems

---

[1] R. Tsunoda, W. T. de Bary and D. Keene, *Sources of Japanese Tradition*, ed. W. T. de Bary, Columbia U.P., 1964, vol. 1, pp. 34–51.

hope to resolve the practical problems of a changing and dynamic society in which competing and conflicting social forces and traditions are constantly probing and testing each other's strength and intentions. In such a society the law cannot model itself upon the Ten Commandments; it cannot limit itself to formal injunctions and prohibitions; it must express the general philosophy that manners maketh man and represent a habit and method of mutual adjustment as the basis of man's life in society.

Mutual confidence cannot strike strong roots if the ground is cluttered by a tangled undergrowth of complex technical detail. Good law eschews technicalities. As legal systems evolve from their primitive origins to their full maturity they tend to strip themselves of technicalities and to rely on broad principles designed to promote and secure substantial justice; the law evolves from contracts to contract and from torts to tort. When formulating new law, for the protection of human rights, in international conventions or in national laws or regulations to give effect thereto, it is particularly vital to deal with large questions in a broad way in this spirit, with magnanimity and courage; only by such an approach can the measure of mutual confidence necessary to make the law an effective expression of the life, and an adequate response to the needs, of the community be created and maintained.

The scope of international action has been greatly widened in our time, but it is not unlimited. We have outgrown hard and fast concepts of domestic jurisdiction, and, encouraged by the foresight of the Permanent Court of International Justice, have learned that as international relations develop whole new areas are inevitably brought within the sphere of international concern and regulation. There remains little in respect of which international inquiry and recommendation can still be regarded as taboo. But the wisdom of international action continues to be limited by the probability of its effectiveness, and the limits of its effectiveness are psychological as well as practical; the frontiers of international action have become political rather than legal but they are none the less real. This is a truth which neither international organisations, nor those who seek their aid in complex situations in which international and national elements are inextricably interwined, can afford to overlook. International organisations can do what they can do for the common good, at any particular phase of their development, only if they neither seek nor are unduly pressed to do what they can not do in respect of matters which in that phase are best left to national action. To apply the principle requires, of course, abundant good judgment and a shrewdness unclouded by illusions, but the principle itself is clear; it is a counsel of prudence, which makes full allowance for the infinite mutability of human affairs, but in no way inhibits boldness within the range regarded as appropriate for international action at any particular time.

Thus far I have indulged in little more than broad generalisations. What, it may rightly be asked, is their practical significance for the contemporary international lawyer? What bearing have they on the manner in which he should advise a government or other client, conduct a case before an international court or tribunal, or draft a treaty or other international instrument? I venture to submit that, as they define the whole climate in which we must approach our task, these considerations are as fundamental as they are impalpable and of vastly greater practical import than the precise authority or relevance of a particular decision of an international court or tribunal or the proper interpretation of some specific treaty provision.

The contemporary international lawyer is confronted with innumerable problems which are either new or arise in some new context; in the nature of things established practice cannot supply the answers to these problems; if we conceive of law as command, and seek to resolve them by recourse to settled rule and acknowledged precedent, we shall be forced to concede that the law has no answers and society is at the mercy of anarchy. Law cannot create the social order, or the sense of community of purpose, necessary to sustain it; it is an expression, not a source, of the values and cohesion of the community; but it is one of the most effective social instruments available to any community seeking to fulfil itself in freedom. It is not inherent in the nature of law that it should perpetuate the past; its function in a mature and dynamic society is to facilitate the process of constant but orderly readjustment to a changing and expanding future. That is the function of international law today, but it is a function which can be fulfilled only if international lawyers approach the specific problems of every day with a breadth of philosophic outlook which situates them in the total picture of the needs and aspirations of our time. It goes without saying that the international lawyer must, like other lawyers, be first and foremost a lawyer, but he is dealing not with the effect of a mortgage, but with the future of mankind, and his vision must be commensurate with his responsibility.

Breadth of view in conception and execution, vigour and imagination in thought and action alike, fearlessness in finding new solutions for new problems in accepted general principles of unquestionable validity, fertility of resource in elaborating new procedures and devices for making such principles effective; these are the qualities required for the successful study and practice of international law today. With them the international lawyer can make a significant contribution to the progress of world community; without them his province will inevitably be limited to the mere trivia of world affairs. Let us be exact, and indeed meticulous, in giving full weight to precedent and usage and resolving legal problems by strictly legal processes of reasoning, using to the full everything which recognised principle and reasonable analogy can offer. Let us by all means be distrustful of general ideas which lack any solid basis in reality. Let us not assume that because much is new all is new, or underestimate the extent to which the basic principles of every major legal system, and the traditional content of much of international law, reflect needs which are perennial in every human society; but let us never forget that all precedents were created before they were followed and, unless the offspring of accident (a poor title to authority, justified only by the convenience of having some established rule rather than none), are essentially an expression of the general ideas of the time of their creation. Finally, let us not reject general ideas which reflect the needs and momentum of our own time because we lack the critical sense and power to distinguish between the perennial and the transitory in the legacy of the past and to reassess the continuing validity in new situations of general ideas and attitudes which the creative minds who left them as their legacy developed as a response to the specific needs of their world and time and would never have regarded as applicable to the changed needs of ours. To face the problem of the future in this spirit is our primary obligation as servants and spokesmen of the law seeking to fulfil its vocation, and the vocation by which it has spellbound us all, to promote and secure the freedom of man in the world community.

These basic intellectual attitudes have therefore an important bearing on immediate practical problems, including the problem which is the occasion of my visit to Tokyo today, that of freedom of association for industrial purposes as a significant issue in contemporary international relations. It is in this broad perspective that we must judge what contribution the common law of mankind should make to freedom, where the line should be drawn between international and national action, what part the international protection of human rights should play in promoting and securing freedom, what role falls to freedom of association among the fundamental freedoms on which the protection of human rights depends, how far the principle of freedom of association applies to the employees of the state and, in particular, to those among them who have a special professional vocation, wherein freedom of association must be tempered by the rule of law and the ultimate responsibility of the state for the common welfare, and what international obligations should be accepted in respect of these complex and crucial matters. All of these questions finally resolve themselves into ultimates.

Do we believe in freedom? Do we believe in law? Do we believe in the orderly evolution of society in a peaceable manner towards better standards of life in larger freedom under the protection of the rule of law? Do we believe that the world is one, and that we are members one of another? If we believe in these things, and have the courage and resolve to translate our beliefs into effective action, all our problems are soluble; if we do not believe in them, then the future of man is bleak with utter and bitter despair. When the question is posed in these terms, the answer cannot admit of any doubt. We all believe in these things and we are going to achieve them together, however long the task may take, whatever claims it may make upon our strength and courage, and whatever reverses and frustration we may encounter on the way. Because we believe in these things, because we have every intention of achieving them, our casebooks and treaty series have some reasonable significance in the broader scheme of things. If we did not so believe, they would be so much waste paper, and much study would indeed be a weariness of the flesh and a burden to the spirit. It is for reasons such as these that the contemporary international lawyer cannot content himself with a practitioner's knowledge of the law. He must find the continuing inspiration which he needs to discharge his task with reasonable adequacy in the deepest well-springs of the human spirit.

9

Due process of law in
international organisations[1]

Those of us who have lived through the growth of international organisations during the last forty-five years have witnessed a remarkable series
of transformations in their membership, their procedures, their authority, their effectiveness, and even in their fundamental conception,
purposes and function.

The League of Nations was designed to supplement the inherited and
traditional political structure of the world; it was to consist primarily of
new arrangements for avoiding any repetition of the breakdown in the
conduct of international relations represented by the outbreak of war in
1914. The United Nations, as originally conceived, was designed to be
a central element in a political structure of the world which was recognised to be changing; but there was little appreciation, when the Charter
was drafted, of how sudden, far-reaching and decisive the changes
would prove to be.

The United Nations has now become the basis, and the only possible
basis, of a wholly new political structure of the world; it has become so with
an institutional framework originally designed for more modest purposes.
These changes in basic conception and function are not matters of
controversial opinion; they are facts reflected in authoritative statements.

The League of Nations was designed 'to promote international cooperation and to achieve international peace and security'; the words
come from the Preamble to the Covenant, but the measures envisaged
for this purpose in the Preamble did not go beyond the fields of political
morality and international law; they consisted of 'the acceptance of
obligations not to resort to war', 'the prescription of open, just and
honourable relations between nations', 'the firm establishment of the
understandings of international law as the actual rule of conduct among
governments' and 'the maintenance of justice and a scrupulous respect

[1] An address to the Faculty of Law of the Hailé Selassié I University, Addis
Ababa, 4 December 1964.

for all treaty obligations in the dealings of organised peoples with one another'. Only in the Constitution of the International Labour Organisation do we find, in the typical international thinking of 1919, a wider and richer vision with a constructive and forward-looking economic and social content still accepted as valid today.

The United Nations was given from the outset a broader mandate, set out in the Preamble to the Charter: not only to 'save succeeding generations from the scourge of war' and 'establish conditions under which justice and respect for' international obligations can be maintained, but also to reaffirm faith in fundamental human rights and in the dignity and worth of the human person and to promote better standards of life in larger freedom. With this end in view the peoples of the United Nations were not only to unite their strength to maintain international peace and security and to ensure that armed force shall not be used save in the common interest but also 'to practice tolerance and live together in peace with one another as good neighbours' and 'to employ international machinery for the promotion of the economic and social advancement of all peoples'. The Charter embodies a pledge by all members of the United Nations to take joint and separate action in cooperation with the Organisation to promote higher standards of living, full employment, and conditions of economic and social progress and development, and universal respect for, and observance of, human rights and fundamental freedoms for all, without distinction as to race, sex, language or religion. Whereas the primary purpose of the League was to prevent great power conflicts and rivalries from escaping the control of diplomacy and degenerating into war, the United Nations was designed for the more ambitious purpose of bridging what we have since come to call the East-West and North-South conflicts; it was, however, so designed upon the assumption that it would operate within the traditional framework of international society, as it existed in 1945, based upon the continuing ascendancy of the great powers granted permanent seats on the Security Council.

The United Nations today has a much more far-reaching role than was or could have been foreseen by 'the most gifted of its begetters': to fill the vacuum in world affairs resulting from the collapse of the old order everywhere, and to provide a framework within which the new political forces of our time can come to terms with each other. There has been no opportunity to formulate this expanded concept of its role in an instrument with an authority comparable to the Preamble to the Charter, but the role has grown out of ineluctable facts and Dag Hammarskjöld gave apt expression to the general concept when, in his last two Annual Reports, he spoke of the United Nations as an instrument for the over-riding common interest of the world community and emphasised the increasing importance of the international executive functions resulting from the process and pace of decolonisation. It is, therefore, a far, far bigger thing that we are called upon to do through the international organisations of today than we could ever have foreseen.

In the context of this greatly widened range of responsibility, the problem of due process of law in international organisations has assumed an importance of the first order for the whole future of mankind. The peace and stability of the world, the rule of law in world affairs, the protection of the dignity and worth of the human person, the promotion of better standards of life in larger freedom, the practice of tolerance and good neighbourliness as vital elements in the common peace, freedom and welfare: the attainment of these primary objectives of international and every rational national policy now depends on the effectiveness of the United Nations and the specialised and regional organisations operating within its framework as instruments for achieving these purposes. Man's stake in peace, his stake in justice, his stake in freedom, his stake in welfare all depend in large measure on the effectiveness for these purposes of the United Nations system, and the United Nations system cannot be effective for these purposes without the rule of law and due process of law.

It is not surprising that the problem should arise most acutely when the world community is confronted with its most intractable problems. Among these the problem of the future of Southern Africa has in recent years come to be of outstanding importance, difficulty and urgency.

Questions relating to South Africa, Portugal and Southern Rhodesia, essentially different in nature but nevertheless interrelated, have become some of the most emotionally charged issues of contemporary international politics and the frustration arising from the difficulty of resolving these problems has produced a wide-spread impatience of due process of law as a method of seeking their solution. This impatience has found expression in the proceedings of a wide range of world organisations, notably the United Nations, the International Labour Organisation, the Food and Agriculture Organisation, the United Nations Educational, Scientific and Cultural Organisation, the World Health Organisation, the International Telecommunication Union and the Universal Postal Union, in all of which the obligation to abide by due process of law has been questioned in varying degrees in the name of natural justice and the overriding claims of morality. It would be tedious, is unnecessary, and would not be appropriate, for me to attempt to recapitulate the precise course of events in these various organisations. In all of them the question raised in varying forms has been that of how far a state which defies, or is regarded by certain other states as defying, the conscience of mankind is entitled to continue to exercise its rights as such in the proceedings of world organisations. The question has become acute in respect of Southern Africa, but it is clearly a wider question which may arise at any time in relation to any state the ideology, policy and interests of which conflict sharply with those of its neighbours or of its rivals on the world stage.

There have been as regards this matter wide divergences of policy among different states and significant differences of practice among different international organisations. It would be neither proper nor helpful for me as an international civil servant to criticise the policy or practice followed by any state or organisation in the course of the exceptionally difficult period of groping and readjustment during which the questions at issue have been coming into focus, but it is entirely proper and may perhaps be helpful for me to attempt to analyse objectively some of the issues of long-range policy affecting the whole future of world organisation which have now been brought into focus and call for long-term answers. Some of the questions which have arisen raise the broadest issues of policy and clearly call for intensive study, reflection and debate.

Among these questions two are of an essentially preliminary character. The first is that of universality versus community of outlook and interest as the basis of international organisation; the second is that of the distribution of responsibility for political matters between the central political organs of the United Nations system and bodies with more specialised responsibilities. I propose therefore to discuss these questions first. The answers given to those questions will determine much of the setting within which the further questions at issue arise.

It is not surprising that intense disapproval of the policy of a particular state should, when deep emotional currents are in full spate and the state concerned shows itself unresponsive to international criticism and unwilling to enter into international negotiation, find expression in proposals to expel the state in question from the world community. By violating the ethics of the community, by challenging and persistently challenging its fundamental values, it almost invites the reprisal of rejection from its membership. But any such proposal raises the fundamental question of policy whether the basis of membership is community of outlook and interest or the need for universality, irrespective of differences of outlook or interest, in the wider interest of the world as a whole. In this respect there may well be an essential difference between world and regional organisations. No regional organisation has any obligation to admit to its membership a state which does not share its sense of common purpose; it can determine how inclusive or exclusive it should be by weighing the extent to which the participation of particular states is necessary for the effective discharge of its functions against the possibility or probability that their participation may dilute the sense of common purpose and reduce the effectiveness of common action. That the Council of Europe, the Organisation of American States or the Organisation of African Unity should determine, and if need be contract, their membership on the basis of such an approach is entirely natural. World organisations are differently placed by reason of their having been established as world organisations aspiring to universality of membership, influence and function; for them any proposal for expulsion, however provoking the circumstances, inevitably raises the question of its compatibility with their universal nature and function. Germs know no frontiers and the vocation to universality which this implies for the World Health Organisation is paralleled in varying degrees over wide areas of international policy. Let us therefore consider some of the issues involved.

I have had occasion to express a view on the problem at three different times, in 1935, 1942 and 1945, the first of these thirty years ago, the last fifteen years before the question became an issue in respect of South Africa. I hope you will forgive me if, in order to detach my views from the context of current problems, I restate them by quoting the manner in which I formulated them years ago during the aftermath of the proposal to expel Japan from the League of Nations and the subsequent expulsion from the League of the U.S.S.R.

My view in 1935 was that expulsion, while conceivably necessary in the last resort in an organisation based on the principle of unanimity if a state in breach of covenant sought to block systematically all League business, was at best a crude device. Quoting Maitland's dictum that 'a ready recourse to outlawry is, we are told, one of the tests by which the relative barbarousness of various bodies of ancient law may be measured',[1] I took the view that

[1] F. Pollock and F. W. Maitland, *History of English Law before the Time of Edward I*, 2nd edn., Cambridge U.P., 1899, vol. 2, p. 450.

a weapon which was at best clumsy, even in societies the units of which were individuals, is quite incapable of achieving any lasting result in a community the units of which are states and one of the characteristics of which is therefore a very low rate mortality.[1]

While particular political regimes have of course a higher rate of mortality than states, basically that remains true today.

In 1942 I was dealing primarily with the suggestion that expulsion might be an appropriate remedy for financial default, but in rejecting this suggestion I commented briefly on the wider issues involved in the following terms:

> International institutions are not clubs from which unpleasant and disagreeable members can be blackballed to the general advantage; they are an attempt to create machinery of government in a world where the unpleasant and the disagreeable cannot be assumed not to exist.[2]

That remains wholly true today.

In 1945, when the present United Nations system was in process of creation, I re-examined the whole question in a broader perspective and ventured to restate the position as follows:

> The effect of expulsion is to release a state from its obligations towards other states under the constitution of the organisation from which it is expelled; such action affords no real remedy for breaches of international law or of international public morality; at best it is merely an *alibi* for the failure of other states to devise effective means of enforcing the provisions which have been flouted; a decision to expel is liable to be taken in a discriminatory manner on the basis of transient political considerations rather than on the basis of the relative gravity of the breach of law and order which has occurred; and it is likely to make vastly more difficult the reintegration of the state concerned into an organised international community when circumstances have changed. Where the continued membership in an organisation of a state violating the obligations of membership would prevent the organisation from fulfilling its functions effectively, expulsion may be a necessary evil; but it should normally be possible to

[1] 'Expulsion from the League of Nations', *British Year Book of International Law*, vol. 16, 1935, 157.
[2] 'Some legal aspects of the financing of international institutions', *Transactions of the Grotius Society*, vol. 26, 1942, 111.

provide for such cases by empowering the organisation to suspend
defaulting members from all or any of the rights and privileges of
membership without thereby releasing them from any of their obligations towards the organisation or producing the long-term political
effects of an irrevocable act of expulsion.[1]

That also remains wholly true today.

I trust I may be forgiven for having disinterred these old quotations.
I have done so to emphasise that the principles involved transcend the
details and accidents of time, place and case; they have a permanent
importance for the whole future of world organisation. These principles
are not stale stuff, no longer applicable to the brave new world of today;
they go to the heart of the effectiveness of world organisation on which
all our hopes for future years depend.

The second question, that of the distribution of responsibility for
political matters between the central political organs of the United
Nations system and bodies with more specialised responsibilites, is likewise fundamental for the future of world organisation. The scheme of
world organisation provided for in the Charter of the United Nations is
one of functional decentralisation within a broader framework of concerted action. The underlying thought is that the world is far too large
and complex to be governed by a world executive and world legislature
responsible for the full spectrum of public policy. The basic policy of
functional decentralisation within a broader framework of concerted
action, so far from being the outcome of a series of historical accidents
or representing the dead hand of the past, is the result of deliberate
decisions of high policy, maturely weighed, which are an accurate reflection of the political realities and technical factors which condition the
present day development of world organisation.

The functional decentralisation of authority in the United Nations
family is an aspect of one of the most characteristic and irresistible
tendencies inherent in the complexity of contemporary civilisation. No
human mind, no tidy scheme of centralised world organisation, and no
network of communications centralised through essentially diplomatic
channels can encompass on the world scale the ever increasing complexity of the interests, preoccupations and problems which transcend
frontiers in the modern world. In such circumstances the functional
decentralisation within a broader framework represented by the United

[1] 'Some Constitutional Problems of International Organisations', *British
Year Book of International Law*, **22**, 1945, 25–6.

Nations system is not a synonym for chaos, but the only workable compromise between breadth of vision and depth of insight, between com-
prehensiveness of approach and effectiveness of impact, between full
responsiveness to centrally focused considerations of over-all policy and
the close and continuous interlocking of international and national
action in particular fields. Upon the success of this wholly new venture
in the art of government depends the possibility of developing an adequate institutional framework for the future conduct of world affairs.
There are, however, certain conditions which must be fulfilled in order
to create any real prospect of such success. As I ventured to put it some
years ago:

> There are, of course, responsibilities fundamental for the maintenance
> of world peace which must be centralised; there must also be effective
> means of evolving by discussion and consent general policies to guide
> the whole international effort; and, if the limited resources available
> are to be wisely used, there must be appropriate provision for func-
> tions more effectively discharged by united than by divided effort.[1]

It is in this perspective that we must consider the problem of how
political questions, and in particular questions with an important and
direct bearing on peace and security, should be dealt with in this decentralised international system.

The original concept was that the United Nations would deal with
political questions, the progressive development of international law,
the general coordination of economic and social policy, and matters not
otherwise provided for. The International Labour Organisation would
promote social justice and deal with labour policy, industrial relations,
social security and similar matters. The Food and Agriculture Organisation, the United Nations Educational, Scientific and Cultural
Organisation and the World Health Organisation would deal with their
respective spheres. The Universal Postal Union would be responsible
for posts, the International Telecommunication Union for telecommunications, the International Civil Aviation Organisation for aviation,
the Intergovernmental Maritime Consultative Organisation for merchant shipping, and the World Meteorological Organisation for meteorology. The Fund and the Bank would maintain monetary stability and
promote investment. Provision was also being made, but is only now
taking a generally acceptable form, for appropriate machinery to deal
with problems of trade and development.

[1] Jenks, *Law, Freedom and Welfare*, 1963, p. 31.

This was and is a rational and reasonable scheme of world organisation; but its workability presupposes that WHO will concern itself with the ills of the body rather than those of the body politic, that UNESCO will educate people for self-government rather than attempt to decide how and when they should become self-governing, that FAO will devote itself to bridging the gap between food production and population increase rather than attempt to determine what political readjustments and changes the increase in world population may involve, and so forth. The eminent meteorologists of WMO know more of the weather than of the political weather; postal officials and telecommunication experts are neither qualified nor authorised to deal in UPU and ITU with race relations and the consequences of colonialism.

If we once depart from the general principle that the responsibility for political matters rests primarily with the United Nations the whole scheme of functional decentralisation on the basis of which so much progress in world organisation has been made during the last generation becomes unworkable. The political organs of the United Nations lose control of political issues. The technical work of technical agencies is disrupted. Within individual governments as well as in international organisations technical departments become involved in political matters for which they have no continuing responsibility and which they are ill-equipped to handle. Chief inspectors of factories find themselves wrestling with riddles for prime ministers and registrars of copyright with the dilemmas of foreign secretaries. The prospect of widespread agreement on dynamic solutions for major problems at the highest levels of political responsibility is prejudiced rather than improved by such a dispersion and dilution of responsibility; the effect is to weaken and discredit the whole structure of world organisation on the further development of which the political, economic and social progress of mankind depends. The purpose of the functional decentralisation of the United Nations system was to take politics out of the widest possible area of international cooperation; a decentralisation which operates in practice to multiply the occasions for political conflict defeats its own purpose and frustrates both the political and the technical effectiveness of the system as a whole.

This does not imply that the specialised agencies of the United Nations are or can ever be political eunuchs unmoved by the passions of the world. The political difficulties and preoccupations of the time will inevitably be reflected in their proceedings; the ILO, for instance, dedicated by its Constitution and the Declaration of Philadelphia to human freedom and dignity, economic security and equal opportunity, can never come to terms with *apartheid* or forced labour. Some of them, notably the ILO and the World Bank, may have important contributions to make within their own fields of competence to the solution of major political problems. None of them is entitled to claim that its field of action is so technical that it should be immune from the political consequences of decisions taken in a proper manner by the political organs of the United Nations. What it does imply is a general recognition that the responsibility for primarily political decisions should rest with the political organs; restraint in raising in technical bodies political matters beyond their competence which have not yet been raised in or are still pending before the political organs; a vigorous use of the proper political machinery for the solution of political problems; and full cooperation in the implementation of the political decisions of the central political organs by the other agencies of the United Nations system. Each of these elements in such an approach is a necessary complement to the others.

Let us therefore assume that our objective in the handling of acute political problems will be to compel rather than to expel and that we will seek to resolve such problems in the appropriate forum, dealing with their political aspects in their generality through the central political organs of the United Nations, seeking the cooperation of each specialised agency in its own field of competence (which may sometimes represent a vital part of the political problem), and securing the cooperation of the specialised agencies generally in making the political decisions of the central political organs effective. What are the further requirements of due process? Four of them are of special importance.

First, each member of an international organisation is entitled to participate in its proceedings through its own chosen spokesman. His person and policies, his past record, present associates, and future plans, do not determine or destroy his representative quality; they may destroy his reputation and influence and forfeit the respect and confidence of his colleagues, but, assuming that a recognised government exists, whether he is representative is a matter for the country appointing him to determine for itself. It is as much a denial of due process to unseat or refuse to sit with a duly accredited representative in an international organisation as for the majority of a parliamentary body to unseat a minority. Any such denial of due process creates a precedent which can be invoked at any time to undermine the political independence of any member of the international community.

Secondly, freedom of speech is an inherent right of all duly accredited representatives participating in a meeting of an international organisation. It is implied in the Charter and by the rules of procedure of virtually all international organisations; it would indeed be a startling paradox if one of the fundamental freedoms proclaimed by the Universal Declaration of Human Rights were to be denied by the international organisations themselves in respect of their own proceedings. Only once in the history of the League of Nations was an attempt made to deny freedom of speech. The occasion was too painful for me to recall it here in Addis Ababa.[1] Without freedom of speech international organisations relapse into the ways of tyranny against which those denying such freedom seek to protest. Freedom has nothing to fear from itself; to allow the evil and the foolish to exhibit the evil and foolishness of their ways is the price of free institutions in a free society. Any arbitrary restraint of arrogance and imbecility also throttles freedom. This has been the experience of all mature political societies; it has a vital bearing on the future of world organisation. There are, of course, no captive audiences in international organisations; freedom of speech is qualified by the freedom to refuse to listen; but when the freedom to refuse to listen encroaches upon the freedom of those who wish or are prepared to hear, the principle of freedom of speech is at issue and freedom itself is in jeopardy.

Thirdly, no state or government should be condemned unheard. The principle is common to all reputable legal systems. Let me quote my old friend, Dr Olawale Elias, the Attorney-General of Nigeria:

> *Aude alteram partem* is as much a principle of African, as it is of English, legal procedure; a popular Yoruba saying is: 'Wicked and iniquitous is he who decides a case upon the testimony of only one party to it.'[2]

Respect for this principle is vital to the authority of international organisations. However reprehensible the policy of a state may be thought to be or may in fact be, it is entitled to have the facts judicially established if it so desires before its policy is condemned on the basis of the allegations of its opponents. It is not entitled to defer political discussion and action indefinitely by a simulacrum of judicial proceedings, but it is entitled to a prompt, full and fair hearing. It is, of course, essential that

---

[1] It was on the occasion of the Emperor Hailé Selassié addressing the Assembly of the League of Nations in 1936.

[2] T. O. Elias, *The Nature of African Customary Law*, Manchester U.P., 1956, p. 243.

the body conducting any such hearing should be wholly independent, completely impartial, thorough in its investigation, and expeditious in its procedure; these are conditions which it may not be easy to fulfil. Where there is a reasonable assurance that they will be fulfilled, to refuse a fair hearing is a denial of due process.

Fourthly, due process requires regularity of procedure. A proper forum, freedom of speech and a fair hearing are important elements in, but they do not exhaust the requirements of, regularity of procedure. The inclusion in the agenda in accordance with recognised rules of questions which it is desired to raise, respect for time limits designed to secure due notice of such questions, the despatch of business in an orderly manner, and respect by international bodies for their own terms of reference and the limits of their constitutional powers are not tedious technicalities which it is legitimate to sweep aside in the name of a higher morality; they are essential ingredients of substantial justice on which all members, whether directly involved in the matter or not, are entitled to rely as guarantees that, before being called upon to participate in a decision which may have far-reaching implications, they will be able to ascertain and give responsible expression to the considered views of their governments or other constituents. There is no place for guerilla warfare in the proceedings of international organisations; its inevitable effect is to disrupt and discredit the organisation in which it occurs to the prejudice of its potentialities as an instrument of effective action.

There remains the question whether these are realistic counsels or counsels of perfection which can lead to no practical result but frustration and despair. Let me put the question in its simplest form: can due process bring results? It can, and due process alone can bring results which will endure.

We must, of couse, recognise that there are certain well defined limits to the possible effectiveness of any form of international action. International action can influence, and in certain circumstances determine, but it cannot replace, national policy and action. What a state does within its own territory is in the last resort determined by itself unless concerted and overwhelming political, economic and if need be military pressure is brought against it by the international community; in practice, this means by the most powerful members of the international community acting in agreement with each other. To change a national policy we must either persuade the state concerned to change its policy or persuade other states to compel it to change its policy; only by due process of law can we hope to do either of these without plunging the world into chaos. Only a programme of change promulgated by due process of law can hope to have any impact on the national policies which it is desired to change; only such a programme can provide the political and moral basis for the concerted and overwhelming pressure necessary to compel changes.

As an illustration of such a programme we may take the Declaration concerning *Apartheid* and ILO Programme for the Elimination of Apartheid adopted unanimously by the International Labour Conference on 8 July 1964. The Declaration is no exercise in idle rhetoric. It is an important step forward for five reasons—

1. it is unanimous;
2. it is objective;
3. it is based on the unequivocal international obligations of South Africa;
4. it is specific;
5. it is conceived at the beginning, not the end, of effective and practical ILO action for the elimination of *apartheid*.

The Declaration is a unanimous expression of the social conscience of mankind, backed by the governments, the employers and the workers of the whole world, not a partisan manifesto but the voice of reason raised above the tumult and promulgated by due process of law. It is a unanimous determination by the International Labour Conference that South Africa has been found, by objective and dispassionate inquiry, to be persistently and flagrantly violating principles in respect of which she has undertaken solemn international obligations which continue to remain binding upon her. It sets forth a specific programme of reform, indicating precisely the changes in labour policy necessary to eliminate *apartheid*, and elaborated in further detail by the ILO Programme for the Elimination of *Apartheid.*

The Programme concentrates on three broad areas, namely, equality of opportunity in respect of admission to employment and training; freedom from forced labour (including practices which involve or may involve an element of coercion to labour); and freedom of association and the right to organise. It concentrates on these matters for four reasons—

1. they are the fundamentals of freedom and dignity in the field of employment;

2. well-established standards approved by the International Labour Conference with near unanimity exist in respect of all of them;
3. the widespread acceptance of these standards in Africa generally, and in substantial measure by South Africa's immediate neighbours in southern Africa, refutes any suggestion that 'the present stage of social and economic development' of South Africa, which is generally conceded to be technically the most advanced of all African countries, precludes their immediate application; and
4. they have all been subject of an exhaustive inquiry by authoritative ILO bodies which affords an objective basis for the formulation of recommendations relating to them.

In respect of each of these matters the Programme sets out, primarily in the form of an analysis of the applicable laws and regulations, the present situation, summarises the findings concerning this situation which have been made by authoritative ILO bodies, contains a proposed recommendation for the amendment of the law of South Africa to eliminate *apartheid*, and indicates specifically the changes in the law of South Africa necessary to make the recommendation effective. The recommendations for action are concrete. They call upon South Africa:

to *promote* equality of opportunity and treatment in employment and occupation irrespective of race;

to *repeal* the statutory provisions which provide for compulsory job reservation or institute discrimination on the basis of race as regards access to vocational training and employment;

to *repeal* all legislation providing for penal sanctions for contracts of employment, for the hiring of prison labour for work in agriculture or industry, and for any other form of direct or indirect compulsion to labour, including discrimination on grounds of race in respect of travel and residence, which involves racial discrimination or operates in practice as the basis for such discrimination;

to *repeal* the statutory discrimination on grounds of race, in respect of the right to organise and to bargain collectively, and the statutory prohibition and restrictions upon mixed trade unions including persons of more than one race, and so to *amend* the Industrial Conciliation Acts that all workers, without discrimination of race, enjoy the right to organise and may participate in collective bargaining.

The Declaration provides for a continuing review of the position by

the International Labour Conference year by year.[1] It concludes with a
pressing appeal to the governments, employers and workers of all states
members of ILO to combine their efforts and put into application all
appropriate measures to lead the Republic of South Africa to heed the
call of humanity and renounce its shameful policy of *apartheid*, together
with a reaffirmation of the resolve of ILO to cooperate with the United
Nations in seeking and guaranteeing freedom and dignity, economic
security and equal opportunity for all the people of South Africa. South
Africa no longer considers herself a member of ILO, but the International Labour Conference has made it clear unanimously that it does
not consider South Africa to have been released from any of her
obligations.

We have failed to secure the cooperation of South Africa, but the
work of ILO to secure the freedom and welfare of the people of South
Africa has only just begun. When all the peoples of South Africa sit
down together on a footing of equality to work out their common destiny
by mutual agreement they will find in the ILO Programme for the
Elimination of *Apartheid* in Labour Matters a starting point for one of
the most crucial parts of their work.

Let me in conclusion attempt to recapitulate the broad principles by
which the international organisations must be guided in attempting to
resolve these vital and complex problems.

The first principle is the rule of law with all that it implies—freedom
of speech, fair hearing and due process. Without the rule of law no
international organisation can protect the weak nor restrain the strong.
Without the rule of law arbitrary action will engender further arbitrary
action and injustice breed injustice. Without the rule of law there can be
no international society at all.

The second principle is that the moral basis of the rule of law is the
protection which it affords to human freedom and the equality of man.
No legal system has ever survived the strains of revolutionary changes
in society without adapting itself to giving expression to what Mr Justice
Holmes so aptly described as 'the felt necessities of the time'. Only by
commanding general acceptance as the symbol and safeguard of freedom
and welfare can the law hold the allegiance of society and avert political
and social disintegration. This is even more true of the world of

[1] International Labour Office, *Apartheid in Labour Matters: ILO Policy
Statements and Reports concerning Apartheid in Labour Matters in the Republic
of South Africa 1964–1966*, Geneva, 1966; International Labour Office, *Third
Special Report of the Director-General on the Application of the Declaration
concerning the Policy of Apartheid of the Republic of South Africa*, Geneva, 1967.

I

international organisation than it is of national societies with longer and stabler traditions.

The third principle is that freedom under law is not a negative but a positive and dynamic concept. The freedom we cherish is freedom in dignity. It embraces equality of opportunity; it includes economic security; it cannot thrive amid hunger and poverty or in a climate of frustration and despair; it is the birthright of all men everywhere, irrespective of race, colour or creed. Any lesser concept of law or freedom will be overwhelmed by the turbulent indignation born of festering injustice and bred by all the forces of evil which batten upon injustice.

These three principles represent the only basis on which an effective and lasting world order can be established; they are the only basis on which Africa can play her full part as an equal partner in a world community founded upon, and dedicated to, peace and justice, freedom and welfare; they are the principles upon which the United Nations system must, and I believe will, always stand.

Our problem today, the problem of the whole United Nations family, the problem of the whole world, is to find ways of applying these three essentially complementary principles simultaneously and with equal vigour. The problem is not one of reconciling inconsistent principles. It is one of so harmonising these three component elements of justice in effective forms of action as to make a reality of the mutual pledges of brotherhood whereby we are bound to each other by the terms of the Charter.

The supreme need of world society is peace; peace requires a universal world organisation the covenants of which are equally binding upon all. The supreme task of world society is to protect and expand the frontiers of human dignity and human freedom, freedom in peace and brotherhood based on the equality of man. This mission cannot be fulfilled, nor peace itself be maintained, without the effective protection of human rights, irrespective of race, colour or creed. Human rights cannot be effectively protected without the rule of law.

The touchstone of freedom is opportunity, the bridging of the gulf between affluence and the frustration of want, hunger, ignorance, disease and despair. The bridging of that gulf requires continuous and concerted international effort to grapple positively with the problem of providing and securing better standards of life in larger freedom. There can be no such continuity of effort without the rule of law.

10

Human rights in a world of diverse cultures in the light of the Spanish tradition[1]

No international lawyer could be insensitive to the exceptional privilege of being invited to address this great university of Salamanca. Salamanca is the birthplace of international law as we have known it during the centuries which have followed the Renaissance, the discovery of the Americas, and the expansion of European influence and culture through-out the world. As we enter upon a new epoch in the history of mankind it is fitting to look back upon all that the European inheritance has con-tributed across the centuries to human freedom and human progress throughout the six continents and the seven seas. Here in Salamanca, Francisco de Vitoria postulated a moral foundation for the law of nations in the principle of respect for the rights of man. Here in Salamanca, Francisco Suarez vindicated his qualifications for a life of scholarship. Here he would willingly have spent the later years during which he elaborated his vision of a world community.

To speak within these hallowed walls is a privilege which cannot leave unmoved any international lawyer with a sense of historical tradition and of the moral responsibility of his chosen vocation. It is a special privilege to come here at the present time, in what I understand to be the year of the seventh centenary of the completion of the *Siete Partidas* of Alfonso the Wise, one of the great law books of all time, comparable in your tradition to Bracton among the common lawyers or to Azo of Bologna among the civilians.

Nor can I forget those who have been your guests before me, James Brown Scott, Georges Scelle, and in particular my compatriot James Leslie Brierly, one of the most inspiring teachers of my youth, who came here in 1948 to discuss the realisation today of Suarez's vision of a world

[1] An address to the Faculty of Law of the University of Salamanca, 10 March 1965.

119

community,[1] in the hope that by so doing he might contribute to revitalising the common intellectual heritage which Spain shares with the whole western world.

My subject this evening is the international protection of human rights seen in the perspective of the historical contribution of Spanish legal tradition and philosophy to the development of international law and of law in general.

International law, like every legal system, is confronted with new problems in each successive age. In the apt words of Rafael Altamira, whose lifelong services to the history of Spanish law and culture were paralleled in his later years by service as a judge of the Permanent Court of International Justice, 'the life of man, like that of every living being, expresses itself in changes and the succession of different states, and his life in the law enjoys no immunity from this common human condition.'[2] Some of these problems, like the prevention of war and the control of armaments, are fundamentally old problems, still unsolved, which have assumed a new and more acute character under changed conditions. Others of them, like the challenge to international action of the problem of economic stability and growth, or the control of advanced technology for the common good, arise from the new opportunities which political and social changes, and the progress of science and technology, have placed for the first time within the grasp of man. Human rights are an old problem to which the experience of the last generation has given an altogether new moral urgency. Our forefathers did not ignore or belittle the problem, but they assumed that it would solve itself with the progress of society towards greater humanity and greater freedom. The problem weighs heavily upon our consciences because we no longer believe in the inevitability of progress. We are conscious, as men have never been before, that our future lies in our own hands. In this perspective, respect for human rights has become a test of the moral viability of society, and of the legal and political order, as it has never been before.

Every great war is a challenge to the moral conscience of mankind. The Second World War was marked, to an extent unknown for centuries, by a 'disregard and contempt for human rights' which 'outraged the

[1] J. L. Brierley, *The Basis of Obligation in International Law*, ed. H. Lauterpacht and C. H. M. Waldock, Oxford U.P., 1958, pp. 366–75.

[2] *Historia del Derecho Español: Cuestiones Preliminares*, 1903, p. 3: 'la vida del hombre se verifica, en todo sus órdenes, como la vida de todo ser, mediante cambios ó sucesión de estados diferentes, y no habia de sustraerse á esta condición su actividad jurídica'.

conscience of mankind'. These are not words of irresponsible rhetoric; they are the measured and solemn language of a unanimous pronounce-ment by the General Assembly of the United Nations. The reaction of free men everywhere to the challenge was as dramatic as it was instinc-tive and healthy. In the Charter of the United Nations the peoples of the United Nations expressed their determination 'to reaffirm faith in fundamental human rights, in the dignity and worth of the human person, in the equal rights of men and women and of nations large and small'. Three years later the General Assembly adopted the Universal Declaration of Human Rights as 'a common standard of achievement for all peoples and all nations'. The preoccupation with the rights of man which goes back to the origins of political philosophy had at last found expression in a recognised international standard defining the human rights and fundamental freedoms which man may reasonably expect the state to respect and preserve and the world community to promote and protect. It is not surprising in these circumstances that the degree in which a state accepts and implements the Universal Declaration of Human Rights should be a significant factor in its influence, prestige and reputation in the world community or that, within the more intimate community of Western Europe, ratification of the European Convention for the Protection of Human Rights and Fundamental Freedoms should have become virtually a required qualification for the admission of new members to the Council of Europe. It may be anticipated that acceptance of the United Nations Covenants of Human Rights, adopted by the General Assembly on 16 December 1966, will, when they have secured the initial thirty-five ratifications necessary to bring them into force, come to be regarded in the same light.

How far is this a reasonable position? Before we can attempt to answer the question we must consider the content of the Universal Declaration, subsequently recast by the Covenants in convention form, and examine how far the principles and values which they proclaim are universal in character or represent the ideology of some particular time or place.

THE UNIVERSAL DECLARATION

The Universal Declaration of Human Rights was adopted by the General Assembly of the United Nations on 10 December 1948. At that time there were fifty-eight members of the United Nations. Forty-eight votes were cast for and none against the Declaration. There were eight abstentions, namely, Byelorussia, Czechoslovakia, Poland, Saudi Arabia, Ukraine, Union of South Africa, U.S.S.R. and Yugoslavia, and two absentees, namely Honduras and Yemen. The United Nations Covenants were adopted by the General Assembly on 16 December 1966 unanimously; there were absences from the vote but all the states abstaining or absent in 1948, with the exception of South Africa, voted positively in 1966.

Though the precise legal nature and validity of the Declaration were left somewhat indeterminate at the time, and have been much discussed by legal writers, there can be no doubt that its political and moral authority have grown with the years. Among the new members of the United Nations no fewer than twenty-three African states have included in their constitutions references to the Universal Declaration or provisions inspired thereby,[1] and the Charter of the Organisation of African Unity likewise endorses the Declaration. As was said by Pope John XXIII in the Encyclical *Pacem in Terris* the Declaration 'represents an important step on the path towards the juridical-political organisation of the world community' for in it, 'in most solemn form, the dignity of a person is acknowledged to all human beings, and as a consequence there is proclaimed, as a fundamental right, the right of free movement in the search for truth and in the attainment of moral good and of justice, and also the right to a dignified life.' The Universal Declaration may still represent a goal rather than an achievement, but we have at least reached the stage at which even those who show little respect for its provisions in practice rarely question its authority in principle. The Covenants, which are not yet in force, are essentially a restatement of the provisions of the Universal Declaration in convention form.

Let us therefore proceed to consider the question of principle on the basis of the provisions of the Universal Declaration. The Universal Declaration spells out in thirty articles the inalienable rights of all members of the human family. I cannot attempt here to recount these in full, but must limit myself to a brief indication of the general tenor of the Declaration. There run through all its provisions six leading themes: the equality of man; due process of law; freedom of thought and expression; freedom of peaceful assembly and association; the will of the people as the basis of the authority of government; and the right to share in the fruits of economic and social progress. Let me attempt to sketch briefly how the Declaration elaborates these themes.

---

[1] The details are summarised by E. Schwelb, *Human Rights and the International Community*, Quadrangle Books, Chicago, 1964, pp. 50–3.

The equality of man

The equality of man is the keynote of the Universal Declaration. The Declaration affirms the principle; insists that it is applicable without any discrimination; and amplifies the obligation of respect for human dignity which flows from it. All human beings, the Declaration proclaims, are born free and equal in dignity and rights. They are endowed with reason and conscience, and should act towards one another in a spirit of brotherhood.[1] Everyone is entitled to all the rights and freedoms set forth in the Declaration, without distinction of any kind, such as race, colour, sex, language, religion, political or other opinion, national or social origin, property, birth or other status.[2] Everyone has the right to life, liberty and security of person.[3] No one shall be held in slavery or servitude.[4] No one shall be subjected to torture or to cruel, inhuman or degrading treatment or punishment.[5] All are equal before the law, and are entitled without any discrimination to equal protection of the law.[6]

The dignity and worth of the human person represents the underlying philosophy on which the whole of the Declaration is based; the dignity and worth of the human person are epitomised in the principle of the equality of man.

Due process of law

Due process of law is the heart of the provisions of the Declaration relating to civil liberties. The concept is set forth in seven principles, all of them fundamental:

1. Everyone has the right to an effective remedy by the competent national tribunals for acts violating the fundamental rights granted him by the constitution or the law.[7]
2. No one shall be subjected to arbitrary arrest, detention or exile.[8]
3. Everyone is entitled in full equality to a fair and public hearing by an independent and impartial tribunal in the determination of his rights and obligations and of any criminal charge against him.[9]
4. Everyone charged with a penal offence has the right to be presumed innocent until proved guilty according to law in a public trial at which he has had all the guarantees necessary for his defence.[10]
5. No one shall be charged guilty of any penal offence on account of any act or omission which did not constitute a penal offence under

[1] Article 1.   [2] Article 2.   [3] Article 3.   [4] Article 4.
[5] Article 5.   [6] Article 7.   [7] Article 8.   [8] Article 9.
[9] Article 10.   [10] Article 11 (1).

national or international law at the time when it was committed. Nor shall a heavier penalty be imposed than the one that was applicable at the time the penal offence was committed.[1]

6. No one shall be subjected to arbitrary interference with his privacy, family, home or correspondence.[2]

7. Everyone is entitled to freedom of movement, including the right to travel abroad, the right to return home, and the right to seek asylum elsewhere.[3]

Effective redress, against the state no less than against the private citizen; freedom from arbitrary arrest; fair trial; the presumption of innocence until proof of guilt; freedom from retroactive penalties; respect for privacy; freedom of movement; these are the guarantees of personal freedom which the Universal Declaration proclaims to be inalienable rights of all members of the human family.

Freedom of thought and Expression

Freedom has its roots in the freedom of the mind. Only where the mind is free and can express itself freely can freedom thrive and flourish. Everyone, the Declaration proclaims, has the right to freedom of thought, conscience and religion; this right includes freedom to change his religion or belief.[4] Everyone has the right to freedom of opinion and expression. This right includes freedom to hold opinions without interference and to seek, receive and impart information and ideas through any media and regardless of frontiers.[5]

It is the essence of freedom of the mind that it includes the right to be wrong; it denies any duty of unquestioning obedience and places the ultimate responsibility for human action upon the conscience of free men.

Freedom of peaceful assembly and association

Man is a social animal. Neither personal freedom nor freedom of thought and expression can give him a full life unless he can share these freedoms with his fellows. Herein lies the significance of the freedom of peaceful assembly and association proclaimed by the Universal Declaration.

The Declaration envisages such freedom in political, economic, religious, educational and cultural spheres. It states the principle in such general terms as to cover all these spheres[6] but, except in respect of

---

[1] Article 11 (2).   [2] Article 12.   [3] Articles 13 and 14.
[4] Article 18.   [5] Article 19.   [6] Article 20.

the political sphere, also reformulates it separately in terms appropriate to each of these spheres. It is in respect of the economic and social sphere that the Declaration deals with the matter most explicitly. Everyone, it affirms, has the right to form and to join trade unions for the protection of his interests,[1] and everyone has the right to own property alone as well as in association with others.[2]

The specific references to freedom of association in the religious, educational and cultural fields are more general in character but nevertheless unequivocal. The Declaration specifies that the right of everyone to freedom of thought, conscience and religion includes the right 'alone or in community with others and in public or private, to manifest his religion and belief in . . . worship and observance'.[3] The Declaration affirms the right of parents 'to choose the kind of education that shall be given to their children'[4] and the right of everyone 'freely to participate in the cultural life of the community'.[5] These are not freedoms which the individual can exercise for or by himself alone; they presuppose freedom of peaceful assembly and association.

The will of the people as the basis of the authority of government

If men are equal in dignity and rights, enjoy personal freedom guaranteed by due process of law, are unburdened of fear by the freedom of the mind, and are free to bind themselves together in fellowship to enjoy these freedoms, they will naturally seek to extend their freedom to cover the whole field of public affairs. The Universal Declaration asserts the right of everyone to take part in the government of his country, directly or through freely chosen representatives;[6] it proclaims that the will of the people shall be the basis of the authority of government; and provides that this will shall be expressed in periodic and genuine elections, which shall be by universal and equal suffrage and shall be held by secret vote or by equivalent free voting procedures.[7]

The right to share in the fruits of economic and social progress

The Universal Declaration does not limit itself to these classical freedoms; it embraces freedom from want no less than freedom from fear and proclaims the right to share in the fruits of economic and social progress by enunciating the right to social security, the right to work and to free choice of employment, the right to just and favourable conditions of

---

[1] Article 23 (4).   [2] Article 17 (1).   [3] Article 18.
[4] Article 26.   [5] Article 27 (1).   [6] Article 21 (1).
[7] Article 21 (3).

work and remuneration, the right to rest and leisure, the right to an adequate standard of living, and the right to education. It accepts the proposition formulated in the Declaration of Philadelphia of 1944 restating the aims and purposes of the International Labour Organisation, which has since been embodied in the Constitution of ILO, that economic security and equal opportunity are essential elements in the freedom and dignity of man.

THE UNIVERSALITY OF THE DECLARATION
AS TESTED BY THE SPANISH TRADITION

Such is the general philosophy of the Universal Declaration of Human Rights; such are the terms in which it applies that philosophy in the broad fields of human equality, civil liberties, the freedom of the mind, political freedom and economic and social advancement. The Universal Declaration describes itself as 'a common standard of achievement for all peoples and all nations'. We have now reached the stage at which we must examine the validity of this claim.

For my part I accept, and indeed profoundly believe in, the universality of the values and principles proclaimed in the Declaration, but their enunciation with impressive unanimity by the General Assembly of the United Nations, while creating a strong presumption in their favour, does not in itself establish that they are valid at all times and in all places. The presumption is further strengthened by the restatement of these values and principles in the United Nations Covenants eighteen years later with even more impressive unanimity. But it remains a legitimate question whether the Universal Declaration and the Covenants represent a synthesis of universal and lasting validity or an expression of a particular ideology, victorious in the General Assembly in 1948 and 1966 but open to challenge in the light of changed or changing political and moral values.

A full answer to this question would require a comprehensive analysis of the legal traditions of diverse cultures in varying stages of their development. Such an analysis would, I believe, show that while the standard set forth in the Declaration has rarely been fully achieved in practice, even in those countries where the rule of law is most securely established and economic and social progress most advanced, the Declaration nevertheless represents an inspiring synthesis of all that is best in the political philosophy and legal thinking concerning the rights of man of a wide range of political and legal systems. To demonstrate this would, however, be a task for many hands and many volumes. All that I can attempt this evening is to trace the relationship between the Universal Declaration and the traditions of which you in Salamanca are the natural and recognised custodians. I hope to show you that, so far from being an alien influence external to your traditions, the Universal Declaration represents a natural expression in the contemporary world of all that western and world civilisation owe to the *Siete Partidas*, Francisco de Vitoria, Bartolomé de las Casas, and Francisco Suarez. Let us consider from this standpoint each of the six leading themes which run through the Universal Declaration, taking first the equality of man.

Vitoria's contention that 'the aborigines undoubtedly had true domin- ion in both public and private matters, just like Christians', and that 'neither their princes nor private persons could be despoiled of their property on the ground of their not being true owners'[1] was essentially an expression of the principle of the equality of man, irrespective of race or creed. The same principle was implied in the advice given to Ferdi- nand of Aragon by Juan Lopez de Palacios Rubios that 'God has given liberty to all men'. We find it again in Suarez's categorical affirmation that the rational basis of the law of nations

> consists in the fact that the human race, into howsoever many differ- ent peoples and kingdoms it may be divided, always preserves a certain unity, not only as a species, but also a moral and political unity (as it were) enjoined by the natural precept of mutual love and mercy, a precept which applies to all, even to strangers of every nation.[2]

Due process of law has still earlier antecedents in the Spanish tradi- tion. The provisions of the Universal Declaration prescribing due process of law all pose the perennial problem of the relationship of sovereignty and law, a question which has been from the earliest times the crux of political and legal philosophy and remains today the heart of the related problems of the rule of law within the state and the effective- ness of world organisation. This problem preoccupied the political and legal thinkers of medieval times throughout the western world, and they all resolved it in much the same terms, by insisting that the authority of the ruler is subject to the rule of law. Seneca apart, the earliest out- standing figure among Spanish political thinkers was Isidore of Seville. Isidore, influenced in part by Cicero and Ulpian and in part by the early

[1] *De Indis*, I, 334.
[2] *De Legibus, ac Deo Legislatore*, Book II, chap. 19, p. 190.

patristic writings, treated justice as an essential part of the nature of the state, postulated the duty of the ruler to do right, and maintained that the ruler should obey his own laws. Through Isidore the concept of natural law, inherited from the ancient world, won acceptance as the acknowledged framework of medieval political and legal thought and the foundation of the law of nations. Six centuries later the *Siete Partidas* of Alfonso the Wise became a classical expression of the obligation of the king to obey the law and the doctrine that the misuse of power is tyranny. The Justiciar of Aragon was one of the earliest examples of a judicial officer whose essential function was to do justice against the state, a kind of medieval *Conseil d'Etat.*

The later history I will not attempt to summarise. I have, I believe, said enough to show that the medieval origins of due process of law in the common law tradition were paralleled by comparable elements in early Spanish law. The provisions of the Universal Declaration relating to due process of law are the fruition in a world forum of one of the oldest traditions which Spanish political and legal thought shared with the whole western world—traditions for which, moreover, important parallels can be found in non-western legal systems.

Freedom of thought and expression has a more equivocal place in Spanish legal tradition, but was implicit in much of Vitoria's reasoning. He presumably did not believe in, and in the nature of the circumstances could not profess belief in, the full freedom of thought and expression envisaged by the Universal Declaration. Toleration as a way of life was born elsewhere. Of course we all bear our share of responsibility for the intolerance and prejudice which has disfigured so much of human history and we all take pride in our own contributions to their elimination; but it was we of the North, your stout opponents of those days, who contributed to the common store of western culture Milton's *Areopagitica*, Locke's *Essay on Toleration*, the oecumenical spirit of Liebniz, the scientific humanism of Spinoza, and the corrosive scepticism of Voltaire; it was we who first translated the philosophy of toleration into a practical reality. The liberal theology of our own day, and the endorsement of the Universal Declaration itself by John XXIII, were still, when Vitoria breathed his last breath, four centuries in the future. But Vitoria, living in the immediate aftermath of the liberation of Granada from the Islamic *jihad*, utterly renounced the whole concept of the Holy War which has continued to poison international relations in our own time and of which the Charter of the United Nations and the Universal Declaration of Human Rights are essentially a renunciation. The refusal of the barbarians to accept any lordship of the Pope furnished no ground for making war on them and seizing their property.[1]

One might say the same today in rejecting the claims of more secular ideologies. Vitoria likewise repudiated the view that the aborigines of the Indies were under an obligation to accept the Christian faith. They were in no wise bound to believe merely because they had been told of the truth of the religion of Christ; their refusal to become Christian after the proposition had been merely put before them did not entitle the Spaniards to declare and make war upon them. In order that there may be a just cause of war those who are attacked must, as Augustine had taught, have committed some fault justifying the attack. The Christian faith had not been so propounded and announced to the aborigines of the New World that they were bound to recognise it.[2] Following Aquinas, Vitoria held that 'unbelievers who have never received the faith, like Gentiles and Jews, are in no wise to be compelled to do so'. The proof, he continued, 'lies in the fact that belief is an operation of the will'.[3] It is perhaps at this point that he comes nearest to the full acceptance of the principle of freedom of thought. War was 'no argument for the truth of the Christian faith'. The Indians could 'not be induced by war to believe, but rather to feign belief and reception of the Christian faith, which is monstrous and a sacrilege'.[4] Nor did infamous vices and morals, or bloody practices, justify the making of war on those guilty of them, or afford a just cause for establishing domination by force of arms.[5] Transposing the argument from the realm of theological to that of current economic and social controversy, it has a highly topical quality and bears directly on one of the most crucial issues of our own day.

The right of peaceful assembly and association lay beyond the juristic vision of the sixteenth-century theologians, but we find germs of it in the emphasis placed in the medieval law books, and in particular in the *Siete Partidas*,[6] on the principle that the growth of *fuero* pre-supposes 'the counsel of good and prudent men (*con consejo de homes buenos et sesudos*)'.

The will of the people is the basis of the authority of government; the principle so restated in the Universal Declaration was formulated in almost the same terms by Ulpian when defining the basis of the imperial authority; we find it expressed with particular clarity and vigour by Francisco Suarez who tells us that civil power in the nature of things

---

[1] *De Indis*, Sect. 2, 357.   [2] *De Indis*, 2, 368–74.   [3] *Ibid.*, 372.
[4] *Ibid.*, 374.   [5] *Ibid.*, 374–9.   [6] I, 2, 9.

resides immediately in the community, and therefore, in order that it may justly come to reside in a given individual, as in a sovereign prince, it must necessarily be bestowed upon him by the consent of the community.[1] The principle is clear; the problems arise when we come to implement it in practice, in the manner indicated in the Universal Declaration, by making effective the reality of representative government. Suarez did not go beyond the principle, but he developed it with a consistency and vigour which was unpalatable to the established authorities of the day. Power, he argues, though residing immediately in the community, is conferred through the latter upon kings or princes or senators, since it is rarely or never retained in the community as a whole in such a way as to be administered immediately thereby.

> Nevertheless, after that power has been transferred to a given individual, and even though it may pass as the result of various successions and elections into the possession of a number of individuals, the community is always regarded as its immediate possessor, because, by virtue of the original act of investiture, it is the community that transfers the power to the other possessors.[2]

An uprising against a tyrant, Suarez considered, 'would not be a case of sedition in the strict sense, since the word is commonly employed with a connotation of evil'. The reason for this distinction was that

> under the circumstances described the state as a whole is superior to the king, for the state, when it granted him the power, is held to have granted it upon these conditions: that he should govern in accord with the public weal, and not tyrannically; and that if he did not govern thus, he might be deposed from that position of power.[3]

That Suarez should have so written demonstrates that the principle that the will of the people is the basis of the authority of government is not an ideological legacy of 1688, 1776, 1789 or 1917, which those with a different historical tradition may be expected to reject, but a perennial element in the moral inheritance of Europe as a whole. The right to share in the fruits of economic and social progress is generally thought of as an essentially modern concept, but for certain of its constituent elements, such as the right to just and favourable conditions of work, we can find clear antecedents in Bartolomé de las Casas and the Laws of the

---

[1] *De Legibus, ac Deo Legislatore*, Book III, chap. 4, p. 207.
[2] Suarez, *op. cit.*, p. 209.
[3] *De Triplici Virtute Theologica*, Disp. 13, *De Bello*, 8, 821.

Indies. Nor has the general concept that the essential purpose of law is the promotion of the common welfare any clearer exponent than Suarez:

> The common good, or happiness of the state, is the final end of that state, in its own sphere; hence, this common good should be the first principle of law; and therefore law should exist for the sake of the common good.[1]

HUMAN RIGHTS AS A FACTOR IN THE RELATIONS OF SPAIN WITH THE WORLD COMMUNITY

The Universal Declaration and the United Nations Covenants of Human Rights are not, therefore, an alien challenge to the Spanish tradition; they are the contemporary expression of the common inheritance which Spain shares with the whole of Western Christendom. Nor is there anything alien to the Spanish tradition in the international character of the Declaration and the Covenants, in the concept that the provisions of the Declaration can increasingly be regarded as the equivalent of international obligations having the force of customary law, or in the increasing tendency to regard compliance with its provisions as a test of reputation and influence within the world community. Permit me one final quotation from Vitoria:

> International law has not only the force of a pact and agreement among men, but also the force of a law; for the world as a whole, being in a way one single state, has the power to create laws that are just and fitting for all persons, as are the rules of international law. Consequently, it is clear that they who violate these international rules, whether in peace or in war, commit a mortal sin; moreover, in the gravest matters, such as the inviolability of ambassadors, it is not permissible for one country to refuse to be bound by international law, the latter having been established by the authority of the whole world.[2]

Four centuries ago the inviolability of ambassadors was regarded as the most natural illustration of 'the gravest matters'. Values have now changed, and respect for fundamental human rights has come to be regarded by the general opinion of mankind as perhaps the gravest of 'the gravest matters'. In a world in which so much is fluid and uncertain, in which the number of independent states has doubled in a quarter of a

[1] *De Legibus, ac Deo Legislatore*, Book i, chap. 7, p. 39.
[2] *De potestate avili*, No. 21.

century, and at least a generation must elapse before the world can adjust itself to so radically changed a political structure and perspective, in which neither the rule of law nor the moral basis of society can be taken for granted, and in which the worship of the power of the state and the cult of material progress remain continuing and ever more dangerous threats to human freedom, none of those who share in the human heritage of western civilisation can reasonably dissent from this scale of values.

The Universal Declaration and the Covenants have another inestimable quality. Because they have been promulgated by the authority of the whole world, exercised through the General Assembly of the United Nations, they can be accepted as a reasonable compromise by widely divergent schools of thought. There have been declarations of rights in a succession of Spanish constitutions, including the Constitution of 9 December 1931, so much admired at the time by legal writers,[1] and the Charter of the Spanish people of 16 July 1945. There nevertheless remains a long-term problem. The acceptance of an international standard, proclaimed as a common standard of achievements for all peoples and all nations, may represent an invaluable contribution to the solution of that problem on a basis acceptable to all.

What, in these circumstances, is the significance of the Universal Declaration of Human Rights and the United Nations Covenants of Human Rights for the future relationship of Spain to the world community and in particular to that more intimate community of West European and Atlantic civilisation to which, by geography, by history, by culture, by economic interest, by political outlook, by strategic necessity, and by moral conviction, she so irrevocably belongs? We cannot allow the question of human rights to remain a gulf between Spain and the western tradition. We must make of it a bridge between them; the common interest, the interest of the whole world, require that we should do so.

It is not for me to say how that result can be achieved. My task tonight is completed by commending the problem for your consideration in the light of all that Salamanca, and the prophetic liberalism of Francisco de Vitoria, have come to symbolise in the history of the law of nations. But perhaps you will allow me to add a few words more in a concluding plea for vision and magnanimity in a troubled world.

---

[1] *Cf.* A. Posada, *La Nouvelle Constitution Espagnole,* 1932; N. P. Serano, *La Constitución Espanola,* 1932; L. J. de Asua, *Constitución de la República Espanola,* 1932.

Might it not be conceivable that Spain, faithful to the moral leadership given to the world four centuries ago by some of her most illustrious sons, and consistently with her approval of the United Nations Covenants of Human Rights in the General Assembly in 1966, might now take some new initiative to give full effect to their provisions and state her willingness to ratify the European Convention for the Protection of Human Rights and Fundamental Freedoms?

Might she not, as an immediate step in this direction, review the position in respect of the international labour Conventions relating to fundamental rights which she has not yet ratified? There are five international labour Conventions which have come to be regarded in the International Labour Organisation as a basic charter of human rights, the Forced Labour Convention, 1930, now ratified by 99 states, the Abolition of Forced Labour Convention, 1957, now ratified by 78 states, the Freedom of Association and Protection of the Right to Organise Convention, 1948, now ratified by 75 states, the Right to Organise and Collective Bargaining Convention, 1949, now ratified by 82 states, and the Discrimination (Employment and Occupation) Convention, 1958, now ratified by 60 states. Portugal has ratified all but one of these Conventions and accepted their obligations in full in respect of her African as well as her European territories. Spain has ratified only one, the Forced Labour Convention, 1930, which was ratified in 1932. Except for the special case of the Freedom of Association and Protection of the Right to Organise Convention, 1948, ratification of which would involve far-reaching changes in the Spanish trade union system, the ratification of these Conventions, while calling for certain changes in current Spanish law and practice, would not appear to involve difficulties of a comparable nature.

If we are to move forward together, in unity and freedom, we must create mutual confidence that we share, and propose to live by, a common faith in the freedom and dignity of man. Let us then so unite our forces to establish and maintain the freedom and welfare of all mankind that we can say with Fray Luis de Leon, another fearless son of Salamanca:

Aqui vive el contento, aqui reyna la paz.—(here contentment lives, here reigneth peace).[1]

[1] *Noche Serena.*

K

11

The equality of man
in international law[1]

'A new nation, conceived in liberty, and dedicated to the proposition that all men are created equal'; so did Abraham Lincoln, in the Gettysburg Address, describe the United States. 'A new world order, conceived in liberty, and dedicated to the proposition that all men are created equal'; so must we now envisage the United Nations. How much happier might the history of the last half century have been if some practicable way of dealing with the matter had been found when the question was raised by Baron Makino, on behalf of the Japanese Government, during the drafting of the Covenant of the League of Nations in 1919.[2]

Those days are now far distant, and the stone which the builders then rejected has become the cornerstone of the new edifice of the United Nations. The Charter of the United Nations states as one of the purposes of the United Nations the promotion and encouragement of 'respect for human rights and for fundamental freedoms for all without distinction as to race, sex, language or religion'. The Declaration of Philadelphia, which anticipated the Charter and now forms part of the Constitution of the International Labour Organisation, affirms that 'all human beings, irrespective of race, creed and sex, have the right to pursue both their material well-being and their spiritual development in conditions of freedom and dignity, of economic security and equal opportunity.' The Universal Declaration of Human Rights and the United Nations Covenants of Human Rights proclaim that 'recognition of the inherent dignity and of the equal and inalienable rights of all members of the human family is the foundation of freedom, justice and peace in the world'; the Universal Declaration further asserts that 'all

[1] An address to the Howard University School of Law, Washington D.C., 31 September 1966.
[2] Cf. D. H. Miller, *The Drafting of the Covenant*, Putnam, 1928, vol. 1, pp. 183–4 and 323–5; and comment thereupon in A. Zimmern, *The League of Nations and the Rule of Law*, 2nd ed., Macmillan, 1939, pp. 262–9.

human beings are born free and equal in dignity and rights' and 'endowed with reason and conscience' and should 'act towards one another in a spirit of brotherhood'.

What are the implications for international law, for international society and for humanity, of this new point of departure? They are more than far-reaching; they are fundamental. The concept of the equality of man has transformed human society during the last two centuries. It has precipitated social revolutions in every mature society. The timing, nature, pace and effect of these revolutions, the extent to which they have interrupted the historical continuity of development, the degree of political and social disorder involved, and their human impact, have varied widely; but law, politics, the economic order and social habit have all been profoundly affected everywhere. Legal privilege for the few has been curtailed or eliminated; political power has been more widely distributed; economic opportunity has been brought within the common reach; social justice has become the accepted touchstone of policy. As United States Secretary of Labor Willard Wirtz has said, 'change has become the status quo'.[1]

During the same period there has been a growing recognition that the equality of man does not stop short at the frontier, knows no ideological limitations, and is indifferent to race, colour and creed. While there may still be found biologists with a special taste for eugenics to describe the equality of man as a 'curious dogma',[2] understandable only as an emotional protest against unkind fate, no responsible person outside South Africa would contend today, as so enlightened, sophisticated and humane a statesman as Lord Balfour did in 1919, 'that it was true in a certain sense that all men of a particular nation were created equal, but not that a man in Central Africa was created equal to a European'.[3] The equality of man has now become a recognised element and consequence of the ideal of human unity. However significant differences of nature and nurture may continue to be, they are no longer accepted as an adequate or even relevant reply to the moral claim for political and legal equality. The validity of this claim is not a matter for biologists, though many of them uphold it; it is a proposition, and has become an axiom, of contemporary political morality. The question is not one of equality of biological inheritance or cultural environment, but of equality of dignity

---

[1] L. W. Wirtz, *Labor and the Public Interest*, Harper and Row, New York, 1964, p. 11.

[2] J. B. S. Haldane, *The Inequality of Man*, Penguin, 1937, p. 23.

[3] See Miller, *The Drafting of the Covenant*, 1928, vol. 1, p. 183.

and rights. We now all concede the principle set forth in the old Chinese novel that 'even immortals begin as ordinary people'.[1]

When we fuse together the ideal of the equality of man and the ideal of human unity we have released the most potent revolutionary force known to history. We have a 'critical mass' the explosive power of which confronts the student of politics with untapped resources of creative or destructive energy. We must choose between the creation of a new world of law and the destruction of mankind. To state the problem, and formulate the principle which must guide us in its solution, does not however in itself suffice to give us the elements of a practical solution.

There is no more difficult and complex problem of social policy in the contemporary world than that of the mutual relations of different races in multi-racial societies. Much of the difficulty of the problem arises from the fact that it is so replete with paradoxes. There is no problem which attracts a wider measure of international attention and no other problem which the societies where it takes an acute form regard as being so peculiarly and intimately their own concern. The problem has both a world history—and it represents a leading thread in the complex warp and woof of contemporary world history—and a special history in each of the societies where it arises. These histories have given an emotional intensity to conflicting approaches to the problem, on the world scene and in particular societies alike, which tends to defy rational analysis. Let us explore briefly some of the reasons for which the problem has assumed, whether we like it or not, the proportions of a world problem.

Why is discrimination a world problem? Why cannot it be regarded as a domestic matter which each country can and should be left to settle for itself on the basis of local sentiment, conditions, and possibilities? Why not leave its solution to those who have to live with that solution every day of their lives? The question is asked frequently, and not infrequently in perfect good faith. The answer, briefly, is that we all have to live with the solution every day of our lives, less intimately perhaps but none the less in a very real sense, because it affects the whole future of the world. We are passing as the result of two world wars within a generation through one of the grand climacterics of history. The political changes of the last twenty years, the repercussions of which are far from complete, have already involved the grant of political independence to some thousand millions of people of widely differing races and cultures in some sixty different countries and their participation in the world

[1] Wu Cheng Tzu, *The Scholars*, Foreign Languages Press, Peking, 1957, p. 33.

community as free and equal nations; developments on this scale cannot be dismissed as incidental to the ebb and flow of current politics; they represent an intercontinental shift of political power and influence comparable to that which occurred when the Americas, Africa south of the Sahara and Asia first came within the effective range of European discovery and influence in the age of the great maritime discoveries of the fifteenth century.

This change in the distribution of political influence among states has been accompanied, over the greater part of the world, by a change in the distribution of political influence within states. Modern education and modern technology have combined to give the equality of man a new importance in the social structure of modern societies; they have simultaneously given a new emphasis to the social claims which the common man expects the economic system to satisfy, made it technically possible to satisfy these claims, and afforded unambiguous proof to all concerned that these claims can be satisfied.

How far has this new dominant chord found expression in the law? Speaking here five years ago Secretary Goldberg, as he then was, said 'the question of genuine, practical equality has been put to law—and the law has responded affirmatively'.[1] How far is the law of nations capable of an equally affirmative response to the question of genuine practical equality? The question was put to law in the recent *South West Africa Case* before the International Court of Justice and the response has taken the form of a decision by the casting vote of the President that the applicants had no standing to put the question. The Court has held that 'its duty is to apply the law as it finds it, not to make it'[2] and that 'rights cannot be presumed to exist merely because it might seem desirable that they should'.[3] It has declined to recognise that a 'right resident in any member of a community to take legal action in vindication of a public interest'[4] is imported into international law by the general principles of law recognised by civilised nations referred to in Article 38(1) (c) of the Statute of the Court. The decision, from which seven judges dissented, has been a severe disappointment to all who believe that the law must respond to and reflect the new spirit of a changed world in order to fulfil the basic social function of providing a framework for orderly change by due process of law in a world in which the choice lies between such change, vigorously pursued, and the utter disruption of the legal order.

[1] A. J. Goldberg, *The Defenses of Freedom*, Harper and Row, New York, 1966, p. 67.
[2] 1966 I.C.J., p. 48.   [3] *Ibid.*   [4] 1966 I.C.J., p. 47.

But one must not lose perspective in the matter. In the *Dred Scott Case* the Supreme Court of the United States found that Scott, as a negro, was not a citizen of the United States and therefore had no standing to sue in a federal court. The law having failed to respond affirmatively, the outcome was the Civil War and the Emancipation Proclamation. The *South West Africa Case* may prove to be the *Dred Scott Case* of the International Court, but it decides nothing, affirmatively or negatively, on the broad general question of the present status in international law of the fundamental principle of the equality of man. That question remains open. Let us therefore examine the extent of its acceptance and the manner in which it is increasingly finding expression in the law.

In this perspective all the great powers, as we would have called them a generation ago, have adopted the broad principle of human equality as a basic element in their general international outlook. Performance may have fallen short of profession, but the acceptance of the principle has been unequivocal.

In the case of the United Kingdom the principle is far from new; it was accepted as the first principle of good government in the heyday of British imperial rule; Queen Victoria's proclamation of 1 November 1858, which remained for all but ninety years the fundamental basis of the government of India, declared that 'all shall alike enjoy the equal and impartial protection of the law' and that 'so far as may be, Our Subjects, of whatever race or creed' shall 'be freely and impartially admitted to Offices in Our Service, the duties of which they may be qualified, by their education, ability and integrity, duly to discharge';[1] this principle became the cornerstone of the Commonwealth as it evolved in later years. In France the Declaration of the Rights of Man and the Citizen begins with the solemn affirmation that 'men are born and remain free and equal in rights' and that 'social distinctions can be based only upon public utility'. French policy derived from this principle 'the conception of the common citizenship, in a united political system, of those of the citizens of home and overseas territories alike who share a common culture and civic life which transcends differences of race and national origin'.[2] The conception of common citizenship did not, of course, survive the transformation of the French community into a group of independent states, but the impact of the Declaration of the Rights of Man on the political thought of French-speaking Africa has been far-reaching

[1] P. Mukherji, *Indian Constitutional Documents, 1600–1918*, vol. 1, Calcutta and Simla, 1918, pp. 432–3.
[2] *Cf.* Jenks, *The Common Law of Mankind*, 1958, p. 238.

and in this respect at least may well be permanent. The Declaration of Independence of the United States of America of 1776 begins with a similar enunciation of principle. 'We hold these truths to be self-evident, that all men are created equal'; there is nothing more fundamental in the political ideology of the United States than this basic principle, and the balance and interplay of political and racial forces within the United States is such that it inevitably projects itself constantly into American foreign policy. Recognition of the 'equality of rights of citizens of the U.S.S.R., irrespective of their nationality or race' is also a basic postulate of Soviet policy, formulated in the early days of the revolution, proclaimed in the Constitution of the U.S.S.R.,[1] and regarded as a key element in the appeal of the Soviet system to the peoples of Asia and Africa. In all these cases we have, therefore, a long-standing and deeply rooted commitment to a principle, coupled with persistent political forces which make it inevitable that that principle should find continuous expression in current international policy.

These concurring, though distinct, policies of the leading powers are reinforced by the intense preoccupation with the matter which exists throughout the extra-European world; notably in Latin America, which has inherited the Spanish and Portuguese attitude of tolerance of racial differences and is confronted with a major problem of assimilating European, pre-Colombian, African and, to a lesser extent, Asian strains in societies which have become, irrevocably, racially heterogeneous;[2] in Asia and the Middle East, where re-awakened nationalisms with their own racial pride have inherited a special sensitivity on the subject from experience of adverse discrimination during the period of European supremacy; and in the newly independent states of Africa. These policies are not, therefore, a tentative or transient phase in the evolution of world affairs, subject to debate, open to reconsideration, and susceptible of modification in the changing contingencies of current politics. They are a response to an irreversible trend of history which has found expression in formal legal obligations solemnly assumed by virtually all members of the world community.

These mutual obligations, expressed in the Charter of the United Nations and the Constitution of the International Labour Organisation, bind us all, in honour as in law. They represent, moreover, an essential element in the new equilibrium towards which, however great the difficulties, enlightened statesmanship must seek to guide the destiny of man. They are no mere gesture of compassion to less fortunate brethren; they

[1] Article 123.　　　[2] *Cf.* J. Vasconcellos, *La Raza Cosmica.*

are an essential guarantee of freedom, dignity and equal opportunity for all citizens of the world community, including in particular ourselves.

There is, nevertheless, a significant gap between this general ideology of current international thought and the hard facts of life represented by the contrast between the affluence of the advanced countries and the pressure of population upon resources in the developing areas. Even more acute than the problems which arise between nations are those which present themselves within nations in communities where differences of outlook, education, habits and standards of life, corresponding to differences in intellectual, economic and political opportunity and maturity, constitute a continuing problem of the utmost delicacy. In the concept of 'equal rights for all civilised men' which Cecil Rhodes conceived to be the only satisfactory basis for the future of Africa, the concept of civilisation is no less vital than the concept of equality. Nor is either concept one of mathematical precision; both admit of differences of approach and of shades of meaning. As with all difficult problems of human relations, timing, patience and moderation are of the essence of wisdom. The maintenance of standards of quality against the impatience of popular pressures has been one of the crucial problems of democratic societies in all ages from the trial of Socrates, through the excesses of Jacobinism which have still left a scar on the politics of contemporary France and the days of Andrew Jackson in the United States, to the problem of contemporary Europe as analysed by Ortega y Gasset[1] or the problem of contemporary Africa; but in all of these cases time has moved onwards relentlessly and brought with it its own compensations. Too much haste may involve less speed in laying solid foundations for enduring progress; but patience and moderation will be swept away by the crudeness of elemental forces if a legitimate preoccupation with timeliness and a legitimate sense of the slowness of natural and organic growth weigh too heavily in the balance against the impulses of courage and generosity which have played a decisive part in all the great events of history. Such are the imponderables which confront national and international policy alike.

Assuming, therefore, that for these reasons discrimination is bound to be increasingly a matter of widespread and profound international concern, how can it be approached internationally in such a manner as to be helpful in the communities where the problem is acute rather than to

[1] See *Rebelion de las Masas* (trans. as *Revolt of the Masses*, 2nd edn., Allen and Unwin, 1951).

make their difficult problems still more difficult? How can we ensure that international action in the matter is guided by a full consciousness of, and acceptance of, responsibility for so dealing with it as to promote agreed solutions and avoid perpetuating disagreement and provoking strife? Unrest may be an expression of divine discontent, but only if the seeds of healthy growth prevail in it over the tares of destruction. As a matter of convenience let us consider separately four different aspects of the equality of man as an international problem, the political aspect, the legal aspect, the economic aspect and the social aspect.

POLITICAL EQUALITY

The political aspect of the equality of man is in its nature the least susceptible of regulation by international law. The most characteristic expression of the contemporary emphasis on political equality is the claim to self-determination for all peoples. Though the United Nations Covenants of Human Rights provide that all peoples have the right of self-determination, it is difficult, as the minority objecting to the inclusion of such a provision has contended, to give any measurable content to such a right. There is no way of defining in legal terms what constitutes or does not constitute a nation entitled to self-determination or when some racial or cultural group not previously regarded as a separate nation comes to be entitled to be so regarded. Why is Burundi a nation, while Tibet and Turkestan are not? Nationality, in the legal sense, is merely the bond between the citizen and the state to which, willingly or otherwise, he owes allegiance; nationhood, which gives to the bond of nationality its real social content, is a cultural rather than a legal concept and phenomenon, and no way has been, or is likely to be, found to assess the validity of a claim to nationhood by international legal process. This aspect of the claim to political equality remains a political matter which can be dealt with positively and peacefully only by processes of political adjustment. The decisive proof that it is being so dealt with lies in the fact that the membership of the United Nations has been doubled in twenty years.

The claim of every citizen to an equal share in the enjoyment of political rights is another characteristic expression of the contemporary emphasis upon political equality. This claim is indeed conceded by the Universal Declaration of Human Rights and the United Nations Covenant on Civil and Political Rights. It does not present the same fundamental difficulty as the claim to self-determination that there is no agreed basis for determining the proper beneficiaries of the right, but as a practical matter few things are more difficult than to redistribute political power and political rights within nations by international action. There is nothing inherently unreasonable or undesirable in attempting so to do, and there may be in the future, as there have been in the past, situations in which international action of this nature is called for and justified by the overriding interest of the peace of the world. But to secure in any general way political equality within nations is hardly an immediately practicable objective of international policy. Paradoxically, it is in some of the countries which have most recently asserted the right to national self-determination that the effective recognition and practice of any real political equality within the nation presents the greatest difficulties.

What then can international law do to give expression to and uphold the principle of the equality of man in the political sphere? At this stage I shall not attempt to answer the question; it must suffice to pose it, before proceeding to consider whether we are yet in a position to give any firmer answer in respect of legal, economic and social equality.

LEGAL EQUALITY

Traditionally the concern of international law for legal equality was a concern for the equality of states. When international law was thought of as a law between 'states solely and exclusively'[1] this was a natural limitation; with the increasing acceptance of the position that 'the duties and rights of states are only the duties and rights of the men that compose them'[2] there has been a shift of emphasis from the political metaphysics of the equality of states to the moral cogency of the position that all men are created equal.

As applied to states the term 'legal equality' embraces and confuses three distinct concepts: that of the equal protection of the law, or equality before the law; that of equal capacity for rights, or equality of status in the law; and that of equal enjoyment of acquired and vested rights, or equality of rights. Of these three concepts, the first is fundamental to the existence of any international legal order. The second concept, as applied to states markedly unequal in territory, population, resources, culture and economic development, is highly artificial and

---

[1] Oppenheim, *International Law*, 1905, p. 18.
[2] Westlake, *Collected Papers*, 1914, p. 78.

has, historically, often been a barrier to the development of effective international organisation based on a realistic appraisal of power and function;[1] it has nevertheless played a recurrent part in the literature and practice of international law through successive generations, is reflected in the reference contained in the Preamble to the Charter of the United Nations to 'the equal rights . . . of nations large and small'. and represents the basis of the composition, voting arrangements and procedure of the General Assembly, the Economic and Social Council, and most other United Nations bodies, but not of the Security Council. The third concept is an ideal not fully realised by any legal system; it is the legal facet of the vision of an egalitarian society.

The new emphasis on the equality in the law of men rather than states has now found authoritative expression in the Universal Declaration of Human Rights and the United Nations Covenants of Human Rights. The Declaration embodies all three concepts of legal equality. It proclaims in terms that 'all are equal before the law and are entitled without any discrimination to equal protection of the law'. It gives a procedural content to the concept of equal protection by provisions relating to fair trial, the presumption of innocence until proof of guilt, and the prohibition of retroactive penalties. It likewise affirms the principle of equal capacity for rights or equality of status in the law. 'All human beings', it affirms, 'are born free and equal in dignity and rights'; 'everyone', it declares, 'is entitled to all the rights and freedoms set forth' in the Declaration; 'all', it proceeds, 'are entitled to equal protection against discrimination and against any incitement to such discrimination'. The Covenants contain corresponding provisions. The concept of equal capacity for rights, or equality of status, has a reality and moral validity in relation to individuals which it lacks in relation to States. However greatly men may differ from each other in gifts, ability and character, their common humanity transcends their differences. Men are equal as moral beings however unequal their biological inheritance or contribution to the common welfare, in a sense in which a major state which has left a mark on the history of the world and a state of a few hundred thousand people which has made no distinctive contribution to human progress are not. The concept of equality not merely in the protection of the law or in the capacity for rights but in the enjoyment of rights also has a measure of validity in relation to the individual which it lacks in relation to the state and runs through much of the Universal Declaration and the United

[1] *Cf.* E. D. Dickinson, *The Equality of States in International Law*, Harvard Press, 1920.

Nations Covenants, notably their important provisions relating to economic and social rights.

ECONOMIC EQUALITY

The concept of economic equality is no newcomer to international law. We find traces of it throughout the development of the modern system. It was an important element in the establishment of the freedom of the seas. It did much to shape the law of international waterways. It gave us the rules concerning freedom of commerce in underdeveloped areas embodied in the Congo Basin treaties, the Open Door policy for China, the General Act of Algeciras concerning Morocco, the League of Nations mandates, and the United Nations trusteeship agreements. It was the origin of the most favoured nation clause in commercial treaties and a wide range of other international agreements.

The concept in this traditional form naturally reflected prevailing economic thought, and this made of it a concept of equal opportunity for the strong rather than of equality. In our own time the emphasis has changed radically. A larger measure of economic equality, as distinguished from equality of opportunity, has become a primary object of the fiscal policy of many states, and this new approach has found expression in the claim that international economic policy should not content itself with securing equality of opportunity but should be consciously directed to the promotion of a larger measure of economic equality. Paradoxically, it is often the states which have done least to achieve economic equality among their own citizens which press most strongly the claim that economic equality should become for their benefit a recognised target of international policy.

How should we envisage the future of international policy in the matter, and how should we expect that policy to find expression in the law? We must clearly strike a balance between what is practicable and what is not, and will find our task greatly facilitated by the fact that this balance does not differ unduly from that between what is desirable and what is not desirable or that between the morally bracing and the morally enervating. It is not the function of international society, and is not the function of international law, to guarantee to all an economic equality which dispenses with the need for the discipline and effort which have created the prosperity of the highly developed economies. It is the function of international society, and therefore likewise the function of international law, to guarantee to all an equality of opportunity sufficiently real to make it possible for reasonable discipline and effort to achieve the degree of economic security and rate of economic progress without which man cannot fulfil himself in justice and dignity. The law can and must play its part in achieving this result. The manner in which it should do so is the great question posed for international lawyers by the United Nations Conference on Trade and Development of 1964. In this context also I must be content today to pose the question rather than to attempt to resolve it.

SOCIAL EQUALITY

At first glance social equality may appear to be a matter of national habit lying beyond the purview of international law. It suggests questions of rank, status and personal consideration with which international law as such is not directly concerned. There has been a revolution in these matters encompassing much of the world, but there continue to be wide divergences of national tradition and practice and in many cases the position is still fluid and the future somewhat uncertain. The claim for a larger measure of social equality has, however, been one of the strongest political and emotional currents of our time and it would be surprising if it had not left some mark upon contemporary international law. It has in fact done so, and international law has developed standards and obligations which powerfully reinforce the current towards social equality.

The story begins with the abolition of the slave trade and, subsequently, of slavery. The concept of a moral responsibility for subject peoples dates back to the origins of modern international law and was prominent in the teachings of the Spanish writers of the sixteenth century, but slavery continued to be regarded as legal by the law of nations until and beyond the nineteenth century.[1] The abolition of the slave trade by the Vienna settlement of 1815, the outcome of British initiative in the aftermath of the American and French revolutions, was the first expression in international law of the new belief in the equality of men. The International Slavery Convention which is the basis of the present-day law on the subject was not concluded until 1926 and a supplementary Convention to make its provisions fully effective was necessary as late as 1956. The abolition of slavery is the first decisive step in the long march from bondage to social equality. By outlawing slavery, international law recognised its concern with the individual and set a precedent for further international action to enlarge the freedom of mankind in a climate of

---

[1] *Cf.* Wheaton, *History of the Law of Nations*, New York, 1845, pp. 585–749.

social equality. In 1815 the powers, on British initiative, abolished the slave trade; in 1919, likewise on British initiative, they declared that there can be no lasting peace without social justice and established the International Labour Organisation to give substance and continuity to this expression of general policy. The work of ILO during the following twenty years made this bold new vision an accepted commonplace and the peacemaking which followed the Second World War developed into a comprehensive philosophy the anticipations of social equality represented by the abolition of the slave trade in 1815 and the creation of ILO in 1919. ILO took a leading part in crystallising the new approach. The Declaration of Philadelphia of 1944 proclaimed what is in essence social equality to be the ultimate criterion of international economic and financial policy, formulating this criterion in the affirmation that 'all human beings, irrespective of race, creed or sex, have the right to pursue both their material well-being and their spiritual development in conditions of freedom and dignity, of economic security and equal opportunity.' On ILO initiative equality of educational opportunity was included among the objectives of Unesco as defined by its Constitution. The Charter of the United Nations gives only a limited explicit expression to the concept but indirectly gives it a wider application; it invokes the equal rights, not of all men, but of men and women and of nations great and small, and it also provides that the United Nations shall promote and encourage 'respect for human rights and for fundamental freedom for all, without distinction as to race, sex, language or religion'. The Universal Declaration of Human Rights and the United Nations Covenants on Human Rights restate the concept with a broader sweep; they proclaim 'the inherent dignity' and the 'equal and inalienable rights' of all members of the human family to be 'the foundation of freedom, justice and peace in the world' and the Declaration asserts that 'all human beings are born free and equal in dignity and rights'. These are not grandiloquent propositions of political and social philosophy devoid of legal content or practical implication; they are the framework of ideas within which a new body of positive law is rapidly developing.

In this new body of law the ILO Conventions relating to forced labour, freedom of association, discrimination in respect of employment and occupation, employment policy, and social security are of crucial importance. They spell out the concept that 'labour is not a commodity' enunciated in the Constitution of ILO and translate the philosophy of social equality into obligations binding states to grant their citizens equality of dignity and status in a humane society. The Forced Labour

Convention, 1930, now ratified by 99 States and the Abolition of Forced Labour Convention, 1957, now ratified by 78 states, guarantee the fundamental basis of social equality, freedom of choice of occupation. The Freedom of Association and Protection of the Right to Organise Convention, 1948, now ratified by 75 States and the Right to Organise and Collective Bargaining Convention, 1949, now ratified by 82 States, guarantee an indispensable safeguard of social equality, the freedom of the weak to associate together against the strong. The Discrimination (Employment and Occupation) Convention, 1958, now ratified by 60 States, seeks to eliminate the gravest barrier to social equality, discrimination in respect of employment or occupation on grounds of race, colour, religion, political opinion, or sex. The Employment Policy Convention, 1964, already ratified by 17 States, is designed to give a more positive content to social equality by the enlargement of employment opportunities. The Social Security (Minimum Standards) Convention, 1952, now ratified by 17 States, which consolidates and revises a network of earlier Conventions with a wide spread of ratifications, provides for a larger measure of social equality in bearing the burdens of accident, sickness, invalidity, old age and bereavement. Considered in isolation from each other and from the general trend of development of international law in our time, these conventions may appear to be of interest chiefly to specialists in social legislation or particular branches of social legislation; considered in the context of the preoccupation with the inherent dignity and equal and inalienable rights of all members of the human family which runs through so much of contemporary international law they become a criterion of the extent to which the state, claiming equality from others, does equality to its own citizens.

These ILO precedents have afforded much of the inspiration for the adoption by the General Assembly on 21 September 1965 of the International Convention on the Elimination of All Forms of Racial Discrimination which is now before the members of the United Nations for ratification. This convention condemns racial discrimination and segregation and propaganda based on racial superiority. It guarantees the right of everyone, without distinction as to race, colour or national or ethnic origin to equality before the law: to such equality in legal proceedings, in the security of the person, in political rights, in other civil rights, in economic, social and cultural rights, and in the right of access to any place or service intended for use by the general public. The International Court of Justice has not yet responded affirmatively to the question of genuine practical equality, but there is an increasingly clear and strong response to this question throughout the range of other forms of international action which must inevitably be reflected in the future development of the international judicial process.

In the process ILO has, as the dissenting opinions in the *South West Africa Case* so fully recognise,[1] been a pioneer: in affirming the principle in the Declaration of Philadelphia; in translating it into an international convention already widely ratified, in the form of the Discrimination (Employment and Occupation) Convention, 1958; in elaborating a detailed practical programme for the elimination of *apartheid*; and more recently in formulating a world-wide programme of practical action for the elimination of discrimination throughout the range of its responsibilities.

In the contemporary world, international action to make the equality of man a reality and not a catchword has become an imperative; such action should and must be unequivocal, but it must also be highly responsible. The equality of man is a world problem; it is, moreover, a world problem of the utmost urgency, a comprehensive and intelligent approach to which brooks no delay; but it is a problem to the solution of which international action can make an effective contribution only if it is based upon a broad and deep understanding of all factors in the problem. In such an understanding historical perspective, a patient but not complacent tolerance of human imperfection and prejudice, and resolute determination to overcome the handicaps of past and present and build the future squarely on the overriding principle of human brotherhood, are all equally indispensable. The problem calls, moreover, for the highest objectivity. Caste and untouchability are no less repugnant than *apartheid* to the principle of the equality of man. Racial intolerance becomes no more tolerant or venial because it is clad in yellow or black than when it is Nazi or Boer. The principle of equality transcends all racial, cultural and religious differences and the obligation of respect for the principle rests equally upon all races, cultures and creeds.

The problem is a political one in the double sense that it has become a crucial and urgent world issue by the operation of political forces and that it can be successfully resolved only by political wisdom. But it is also essentially a practical problem in the sense that while the guide to its solution must be found in principle, and fundamentally in moral principle, it resolves itself in practice into a series of practical questions.

[1] Wellington Koo, V.-P., 1966, I.C.J., at pp. 226–7; Judge Tanaka, J. *ibid.*, at p. 252, Jessup, J., *ibid.*, at pp. 374, 377 and 416–17 and Padilla Nervo, J., *ibid.*, at p. 468.

The problem of discrimination in respect of employment, for instance, resolves itself into a series of such questions as opportunities for and methods of training, human relations and methods of communication in industry, comparative standards of life, wages policies, conditions of work and social security. Only by a comprehensive and intensive effort to deal on their merits with each of these elements in the complexities of contemporary social problems can we hope to remove the issue of discrimination from the dangerous arena of emotional generalities to the constructive tasks of solid political, economic and social progress. Only by such an approach can we build the common law of mankind on the basis of the equality of man.

Let me conclude, as I began, with Lincoln: 'The dogmas of the quiet past are inadequate to the stormy present. The occasion is piled high with difficulty and we must rise to the occasion.'[1] If we fail to respond affirmatively to the challenge of a genuine practical equality we will discredit beyond repair the part which the law can play in creating a world community of freedom and justice.

[1] Message to Congress, 1 December 1864.

12

The open society and international law[1]

There is no ideal to which the western world is more firmly and rightly attached than that of an open society. It embodies all that is best in our political traditions, our social temper, and our moral upbringing. The open society has always had its enemies; it has its enemies today. It has had, and has, its enemies without, and its enemies within. Throughout history it has been wrestling with the dilemma of overcoming its enemies, without and within, without compromising its own traditions, the vitality of its own ideals, and the integrity of its own moral purpose; it still wrestles with that dilemma today.

International law is not foreign to these issues; it does not belong to a world apart, in which states conduct their mutual relations without regard to their political and social ideals. International law was born on the battlefield; it operates today on a battlefield of ideas and interests where titans are warring for mastery. In this context, what is its potential contribution to the open society of our ideals, the professed purpose of all our political strivings? Before we can attempt to answer, we must first consider what we mean by an open society.

We mean a society in which men are free to think and speak and write as they choose; in which they can associate together as free men for political and economic and cultural purposes; in which the government of the people is conducted by the people and is subject at all times to the will of the people expressed through free elections and a free press. We mean a society in which men are free to worship God in their own way; in which all intolerance has been discarded; and in which all human beings, irrespective of race, creed or sex, are no less equal in the lives of their fellows than in the sight of God. We mean a society in which men are free from fear; in which peace no longer depends on a balance of nuclear terror; in which there is no arbitrary arrest, detention or exile,

[1] An address at the Northwestern University School of Law, Chicago, 1 February 1965.

no cruel or unusual punishment, no retroactive penalty or guilt by association; and in which there is no slavery, forced labour, *apartheid* or other racial discrimination. We mean a society in which men are free from want; in which the war against poverty is being pressed to a successful conclusion by combined national and international action; in which the gap between affluence and indigence is being narrowed by far-sighted economic and social policies equally concerned with increasing productivity and a more equitable distribution of the product; in which the growth of the population is no longer constantly threatening to out-strip the expansion of usable resources. We mean a society in which scientific and technological progress is harnessed to the service of these freedoms.

These freedoms are not the claims of long-haired idealists. They are the birthright of free Englishmen and free Americans. They can be traced back to Magna Carta. Most of them are proclaimed in the Declaration of Independence, the Constitution of the United States, and the Bill of Rights. They are all enshrined in the Universal Declaration of Human Rights and the United Nations Covenants of Human Rights. Their preservation and expansion was the professed purpose and policy of the western powers in the greatest war of history. They have been constantly reaffirmed by governments with the most varied outlooks and policies.

There is nothing stale in the four freedoms as Franklin Roosevelt enunciated them a quarter of a century ago. 'Age shall not wither them', nor triteness freeze their infinite vitality. All that has happened in the world since that time has confirmed their permanent importance. The cold war and decolonisation have given them a new urgency. They are perhaps the most important legacy of the age of western supremacy to the non-western world. With them we can move forward to win for all men everywhere a lasting inheritance of freedom and dignity, made possible by a secure peace, based on equal opportunity, buttressed by economic security and growth, fostered by scientific and technological advance, and devoted to the boundless quest of the human spirit for truth, beauty and brotherhood.

What part can we expect the law to play in this, the great adventure of our time? Is it indeed any business of the law to concern itself with such high matters, or should it be content to deal with the humbler mishaps of everyday life? Can the law play, should it play, so ambitious a part in even the most developed legal systems? How can it possibly play such a part in the infinitely more difficult arena of international relations? Does not the history of the last twenty years show how complete is any such illusion?

I am not so sceptical of the part which the law can play; I believe that it can, that it must, and that it will, serve as one of the indispensable instruments for the attainment of these aims. I believe that it is one of the primary responsibilities of contemporary international lawyers to fit themselves to play their part in the great forward movement of humanity. Our function is not to perpetuate the past but to create the future; not to entrench the sovereignty of the state but to build the *civitas maxima* of mankind; not to exalt the politics of power but to expand the healing influence of justice; not to harden, deepen and embitter ideological mistrust, controversy and conflict, but to mellow, and restore the freedom of initiative and innovation of, far-sighted constructive statesmanship.

Only a living law can meet the needs of a living society. The legal history of political and social conflict in national societies has much to teach us concerning the crucial problems which confront international lawyers today. Law has never resolved political or social conflict by invoking the past to imprison the future; it becomes an important contributory solvent of such conflict only when it draws upon the heritage of the past to enable the present to foresee the needs of the future.

Approaching the matter in this spirit, what must international law enable us to do, what must we do through international law, if the purposes which we have recognised to be implicit in the concept of the open society are to be achieved? What, in short, do we require of the law, as the handmaiden and instrument of policy, in order that we may fulfil these aims and purposes? It must, in the world of today, do at least seven things:

1. It must preserve us against the dangers of nuclear war.
2. It must enable societies with widely divergent ideas and interests to coexist in freedom.
3. It must provide effective means of settling international disputes.
4. It must afford reasonable opportunity for peaceful changes in the existing order of things.
5. It must furnish an appropriate legal framework for a buoyant and expanding world economy.
6. It must protect the rights of man.
7. It must ensure that scientific and technological change remains our servant and does not become our master.

Clearly the law alone can do none of these things; they are all challenges to the highest statesmanship. But equally clearly statesmanship can achieve none of these things without using the law as one of its instruments for the purpose. One of the crucial tests of contemporary statesmanship is whether it is prepared to use, and is successful in using, an expanding rule of law to achieve these purposes. The crucial test of contemporary legal scholarship and craftsmanship is whether it is prepared and able to place itself effectively at the service of statesmanship to this end. These are not days in which the scholar can escape commitment. When we are confronted with tasks of this magnitude, he that is not for us is against us. The ivory tower is the death cell of moral integrity in so challenging a world; but there is no integrity in catchwords unsuspectingly borrowed from an alien dialect. All of these problems call for a rigorous analysis of what is desirable and practicable in a divided world. All of them call for clear and hard thinking and the firm rejection of slogans designed to mask rather than to illuminate reality. All of them call for initiatives and persistence of altogether new proportions; it will not suffice to do what we are doing but do it rather better. Let us consider them in turn.

Statesmanship, using the law as one of its instruments, must preserve us against the dangers of nuclear war. It is not sufficient that war is no longer legal, or that nuclear tests in the atmosphere, under water and in outer space have been banned. Before we can breathe freely we must be reasonably assured: that the commitment that force shall not be used save in the common interest undertaken by all the members of the United Nations under the Charter will be loyally observed; that we have established a system of arms control sufficiently comprehensive in coverage and effective in practice to avert the danger of subjugation by surprise; that effective precautions have been taken, by hot lines or otherwise, to minimise the danger of escalation into war by misunderstanding or panic; and that aggression, if it occurs, will be promptly and effectively restrained by the collective action of peace and freedom loving peoples without precipitating a nuclear holocaust. Until these conditions have been fulfilled we shall have failed to discharge our responsibility to make a solid reality of the renunciation of war.

The outlawry of war was born here in Chicago. The General Treaty for the Renunciation of War and the Charter of the United Nations have made it the foundation of contemporary international law. It remains to complete the task of making it a political reality; how shall we so bind up the wounds of the past as to make this possible?

Statesmanship, using the law as one of its instruments, must enable societies with widely divergent ideas and interests to coexist in freedom. Coexistence has become a suspect concept in the west, and no doubt the expression has been so tortured in meaning in some quarters that it is well to receive it with caution into, and treat it with reserve in, the accepted vocabulary of international law and diplomacy. But, stripped of emotional exegesis, coexistence, in its literal meaning, is the essence of all human society, and without it there can be no world community for ourselves, our children, or our children's children. We would therefore be more profitably employed in giving to the concept a real and acceptable content than in rejecting it as the worship of false gods. Coexistence, in any reasonable sense of the term, implies the frank and genuine acceptance of continuing diversity, the will to live with each other rather than to bury each other, and the acceptance of due process of law for the adjustment of conflicting interests. To coexistence in this sense we are all pledged by the terms of the Charter, which states the common determination of the peoples of the United Nations 'to practise tolerance and live together in peace with each other as good neighbours'.

How are we, as good neighbours, to compose our differences? Statesmanship, using the law as one of its instruments, must promote effective means of settling international disputes. The efforts and experience of the last 170 years have given us the instruments for this purpose. International arbitration has developed into judicial settlement. We have an International Court of Justice, now so composed as to be fairly representative of the whole world and of the highest authority. We have in the United Nations a wide range of alternative procedures for the adjustment of disputes for which a political settlement is preferred by some or all of the parties involved. The problem is no longer one of creating means of settlement but one of ensuring full and prompt use of the means available with a genuine desire to succeed. Such a desire can be effective only if it is general; there must be a willingness on all sides to make the mutual concessions necessary to success. But the general will is rarely a spontaneous birth. It needs to be fertilised by a seminal force of abundant vitality. Without bold and strong leadership by those with the moral authority and political power to give such leadership there will be little hope of progress.

Imaginative and aggressive leadership in the promotion of peaceful settlement is urgently necessary in the political and judicial spheres alike. The two approaches are complementary to each other and there is nothing to be gained by debating their relative priority and importance. The matter is one not of principle but of practical wisdom; so much depends on time, place and circumstance. But international lawyers have a special responsibility in respect of the judicial sector. Without a substantial element of compulsory jurisdiction the rule of law will inevitably be precarious, and none of us can complain of the unwillingness of others to accept compulsory jurisdiction while we ourselves retain the right to decline such jurisdiction in respect of matters of domestic jurisdiction as determined by ourselves.

In this perspective a wider acceptance of the Optional Clause of the Statute of the International Court, unaccompanied by a reservation of matters of domestic jurisdiction as determined by the party concerned, would be an important step towards giving greater reality to the obligation under the Charter to settle international disputes by peaceful means. A powerful state can no longer secure justice for itself by the strength of its own right arm without so transgressing the modern law of nations and so offending the ethos of contemporary international society that it is almost bound to lose far more in general prestige and influence than it can hope to gain in the particular case. The days when the compulsory jurisdiction of international courts and tribunals was primarily a protection for the weak which it was natural for the strong to resent and attempt to evade have passed; for strong and weak alike there is now no effective redress for the victim of injustice except due process of law; only if we are convinced that we will be more sinners than sinned against have we a continuing interest in rejecting compulsory jurisdiction. In these circumstances, what have we to fear from vigorous initiative?

The basis of compulsory jurisdiction is reciprocal obligation. If others do not choose to follow whatever lead we may give, wherein are we the losers? The common task remains uncompleted, but our part at least has been done and by doing it we will have made it more probable that a broader acceptance of compulsory jurisdiction will ultimately be achieved.

We must never, however, cherish the illusion that compulsory jurisdiction alone will provide a satisfactory means of resolving all the international disputes of a world in travail. Statesmanship, using the law as one of its instruments, must also afford reasonable opportunity for peaceful changes in the existing order of things—in the political order and in the economic order—which go well beyond the maximum scope for judicial reinterpretation of the law and readjustment of existing

rights in the most dynamic of legal systems. Peaceful change is primarily
a political rather than a legal problem, much as legislative policy is more
a matter of policy than of law. In no period of history has there been
more peaceful change than in recent years. It has been made possible
primarily by the widespread recognition of the inevitability of change,
but nothing is more difficult than to institutionalise the processes of
change. Any precise institutionalisation of procedures of change is unattainable, and perhaps undesirable, but change in an organised society
in which all the resources of social organisation can be and are deployed
as appropriate to facilitate and make adjustments to change is a totally
different matter from the convulsive violence which is so often typical of
change in a less organised society. Within the general framework of the
United Nations there are important possibilities of this nature previously
unknown or undeveloped. The constant reassessment and reformulation
of policy as the result of discussions in the General Assembly, the Coun-
cils, the regional commissions and other bodies and conferences plays an
important part. The habit of negotiation, by quiet diplomacy or otherwise, gradually becomes a more settled one.

    Judicially conducted inquiries not limited to establishing the facts or
the law but designed to provide an objective basis for future policy may
prove to be increasingly important; they may serve to introduce an
element of reasonable evaluation into conflicts which have become irrat-
ional, enable all the parties to take a fresh look in a changed perspective
at the different elements in the problem, and thereby provide a new
point of departure from which an equitable readjustment of existing
rights, interests and policies becomes possible. The law-making treaty
serves as a device for giving legal form and force to new settlements. New
types of international bodies are more easily created to administer such
settlements. Such bodies can be given certain discretionary powers to
adapt the settlement adopted to future needs. In all these respects the
more vigorous development of world organisation facilitates peaceful
change.

    Change is more likely to be generally acceptable when the economy is
buoyant and expanding. Statesmanship, using the law as one of its
instruments, must furnish an appropriate framework for a buoyant and
expanding world economy. The concept of collective security which
crystallised as the result of the First World War has now been expanded
into that of collective economic security. So wide are the divergences of
economic interest and philosophy among the nations that it has been a
difficult birth, but with the United Nations Trade and Development

Conference of 1964 we have reached a point of no return. What measure of obligation the more advanced nations should assume to foster economic growth elsewhere, and in what manner such obligations as they may recognise should be discharged, are among the most difficult of our current problems. They cannot be resolved by expressing as the decision of a majority the claims and ambitions which the have-nots wish to give notice of to the haves. A wide consensus born of a sense of mutual responsibility for the common good by conflicting interests represents the only possible basis for effective action. We need, and need urgently, procedures of discussion and negotiation designed to facilitate such a consensus; and once we have created such procedures we must use them with bold imagination to ensure monetary stability and avert inflation, to maintain equitable terms of trade, to secure a reasonable return to primary producers, and to promote a high level of investment on fair terms. These preoccupations are a far cry from diplomatic immunities or jurisdiction over merchant ships in port in criminal matters but they represent an increasingly important proportion of the contemporary law.

The law must be a framework for prosperity, but for prosperity in freedom. Statesmanship, using the law as one of its instruments, must protect the rights of man. The Universal Declaration of Human Rights, promulgated by the General Assembly in 1948 as a common standard of achievement for all peoples and all nations, has blazed the trail; in the absence of any more binding international obligations of comparable universality and scope it tended, by general consent, to fill the void and to acquire an accretion of customary authority progressively hardening into law. But for eighteen years it was only in ILO, which administers widely-ratified conventions prohibiting forced labour, guaranteeing freedom of association, and providing for the elimination of discrimination in employment, and in Western Europe, where the European Convention for the Protection of Human Rights and Fundamental Freedoms gives a watching brief for the enforcement of civil liberties to the European Commission of Human Rights and provides for their enforcement by the European Court of Human Rights and the Committee of Ministers of the Council of Europe, that any significant progress was made in the formal acceptance of binding international obligations to respect the rights of man and the development of procedures designed to ensure that the obligations formally accepted are effective in practice.

The unanimous approval by the General Assembly in 1966 of the United Nations Covenants on Economic, Social and Cultural Rights and on Civil and Political Rights opens up a vastly enlarged perspective of possible world-wide action in the matter, but the practical value of the Covenants will depend on the extent to which they are widely and promptly ratified without reservations which detract significantly from the obligations which they embody and on the manner in which the procedures of implementation for which they provide are applied. If we still believe in the English, American and French revolutions, and still regard 1688, 1776 and 1789 as landmarks in the history of human freedom, we will not hesitate to be the leaders in a world-wide movement to enshrine the rights of man in the fundamental law of the world community and to provide for their effective enforcement by international procedures. No sane man wishes international busybodies to take over the responsibilities of local magistrates, but, subject to appropriate safeguards against the abuse of international procedures, there is a real need for arrangements which ensure that the writ of human freedom runs everywhere. Only those who are prepared to accept service of that writ themselves have any moral claim to serve it upon others. Therein lies the case for the acceptance of international obligations in respect of human rights by all who believe that their own record in respect of human rights defies comparison.

The challenge to the law of the progress of science and technology poses a similar problem. Statesmanship, using the law as one of its instruments, must ensure that scientific and technological change remains our servant and does not become our master. There is a special temptation for advanced and powerful states to value their freedom of action on the frontiers of scientific and technological progress, and reject as premature any legal regulation which may deprive them of some possible advantage which their resources or skills may place within their reach. Such an attitude represents a short view of one of the fundamental problems of our time. No state, no matter how great may be the lead which it may appear to have at any particular time, has any monopoly of the resources and skills which are the raw material of scientific and technological ascendancy. The gamble of freedom of action may or may not pay off for one or other of the leading contenders, but only in the discipline of law can there be any common or lasting security. Only by entering into firm international obligations governing nuclear energy, activities in space and the modification of natural environment can we all enjoy reasonable protection against the dangers to our lives and liberties implicit in the race for nuclear and space ascendancy. The Partial Nuclear Test Ban Treaty and the Treaty on Principles Governing the Activities of States in the Exploration and Use of Outer Space, including the Moon and Other Celestial Bodies, are important steps in this direction.

Let us now recapitulate the succession of challenges which has emerged from our analysis. Are we prepared to seek peace and pursue it as the overriding objective of international policy? Are we prepared loyally to maintain our commitment under the Charter of the United Nations that force shall not be used save in the common interest? Are we prepared so to control arms by law that they cease to be a constant challenge to, and become the disciplined weaponry of, the law?

Are we prepared to unite our strength with that of other peace and freedom loving peoples effectively to prevent and restrain aggression? Are we prepared, while remaining vigilant in preserving our own freedom and security, to practice tolerance and live together as good neighbours with those with whom we disagree, even as regards fundamentals?

Are we prepared to accept the compulsory jurisdiction of international courts and tribunals, without any reservation of domestic jurisdiction as determined by ourselves? Are we prepared to develop international procedures for changing vested rights in an orderly manner on grounds of equity and public policy? Are we prepared to accept, in the fields of currency, trade and commodity policy, and investment, firm international obligations which will underpin a buoyant and expanding world economy? Are we prepared to enter into firm international obligations to maintain and protect civil liberties and economic social rights and to create effective procedures to make a reality of these obligations? Are we prepared to enter into firm international obligations governing nuclear energy, activities in space, the modification of natural environment, and the other current achievements of advanced technology?

These are the acid tests of the extent and sincerity of our commitment to our professed ideals. Only when we pass these tests will we be entitled to speak proudly of a new world of law. If our faith in the open society is full-blooded we must and will be prepared to do all these things. If we are not prepared to do them, let us not cast the first stone at our neighbours but seek some empirical basis on which we can all move in the general direction of these objectives. The task is not for today, nor for tomorrow, but for all time. But let us at least try to keep moving in the right direction.

Index

'*ādat* law, 85
adjudication, international, 10–11, 26–7, 60–1, 154–5
African Development Bank, 75
agenda for dialogue on growth of law, 4
aggression, restraint of, 61, 68–70, 153
aims and purposes of legal order, 100–1, 117–18, 131, 151–2
Alfonso the Wise, 119, 128
Alisjahbana, S. T., 86
Alliance for Progress, 75
Altamira, Rafael, 120
Ananthanarayanan, Chief Justice, 67
Aquinas, Thomas, 129
Aristotle, 31
armament, control of, 59–60, 153
armed force, restraint of, 24–5, 58, 90–91, 153
Asian Development Bank, 75, 92
audi alteram partem, 113–14
Azo of Bologna, 119

Balfour, Lord, 135
Bank for International Settlements, 75
Blackstone, William, 87
Bracton, 87, 119
Brierly, James Leslie, 119

change, effect on law, 1–3, 15, 36, 42–5, 53–5, 57, 65, 85–7, 94–5, 100–1, 135, 155–6
Chinese attitude to law of nations, 88
Chinese tradition and the legal order, 84–5
Chosroes, 43
Cicero, 127
co-existence, 14, 19–23, 91–2, 154
Coke, Sir Edward, 87
collective security, 61, 68–71
Colombo Plan, 75
commodity policy, 63
compliance with international decisions, 14, 73–4
compulsory jurisdiction, 10–11, 26–7, 37, 60–1, 154–5

concept of law, 4–5
Congo Basin treaties, 144
consensus, 81–2, 97–8, 157
Constitution of the United States, 151
consultation, obligations of, 79–81
corporate personality for international purposes, 45–51
Cospar, 81
Council of Europe, 41, 107
Council of Mutual Economic Assistance, 41
currency, 63, 74–5, 80
custom, 8–9
Cyrus, 43

Dante, 34
Darius, 43
Declaration of Independence of the United States, 139, 151
Declaration of Legal Principles Governing the Activities of States in Space, 13, 29, 78, 81
Declaration of the Rights of Man and the Citizen, 89, 138
defamation, 90
discrimination, 89, 115–18, 123, 134–149
Dred Scott Case, 137–8
due process of law, 123, 127–8
due process in international organisations, 13, 103–18

ecological balance, 39
economic equality, 144–5
economic stability and growth, 37–8, 62–3, 74–8, 144–5, 156–7
Elias, Olawale, 113
equality of man, 123, 134–49
equity, 9–10
escalation, safeguards against, 60, 155
ethical pillars of law, 3
European Convention for the Protection of Human Rights and Fundamental Freedoms, 28, 121, 132, 157
European Economic Community, 80

European Free Trade Association, 80
European Launcher Development
Association, 79
European Payments Union, 74
European Recovery Programme, 75,
76
European Space Research Organisa-
tion, 79
expulsion from world organisations,
18–19, 106–9

Ferdinand of Aragon, 127
Fitzmaurice, Sir Gerald, 48, 55
Food and Agriculture Organisation,
105, 110, 111
Frankenstein, 34
freedom as vocation of law, 95–7
freedom of association, 101–2, 115–16,
124
freedom of information, 89–90
freedom of speech, 113, 124, 128
freedom of thought, 17, 124, 128–9

General Act of Algéçiras, 144
General Agreement on Tariffs and
Trade, 38, 76
general principles of law, 9
General Treaty for the Renunciation
of War, 153
general welfare as legal interest, 52–3
Global Communications Satellite
System, 79–81
Goldberg, Arthur J., 137
good faith, 3, 25
good-neighbourliness, 90–93
Grotius, Hugo, 6
growth of law, 3–13, 44–5

Hague Peace Conferences, 27
Hailé Selassié, H.M. Emperor, 113
Hammarskjöld, Dag, 40
Hegel, G. W. F., 32
Heraclitus, 55
Hobbes, Thomas, 33
Holmes, O. W., Jr., 41, 48, 117
human rights, 26–7, 37, 53, 61–2, 98,
101–2, 119–33, 157–8

ideological differences, 1–2, 16–17,
19–21, 58, 126
Indus Waters Treaty, 76
information, freedom of, 89–90

intellectual freedom, relation to rule
of law, 17, 124
Inter-American Development Bank,
75
Intergovernmental Maritime Consultative Organisation, 111
international action, limitations of,
99–100, 114–15
International Bank for Reconstruc-
tion and Development, 63, 75, 76,
110, 112
International Civil Aviation Organisation, 110
International Court of Justice, 27, 44,
45, 46, 48, 53, 73, 147, 148,
154–5
*Certain Expenses of United Nations
Case*, 48
Northern Cameroons Case, 48
Reparation for Injuries Case, 48–9
South West African Cases, 44–5, 48,
52, 53–4, 87, 137, 138, 148
U.N. Administrative Tribunal Case,
48
International Development Associa-
tion, 75
International Finance Corporation, 75
International Labour Organisation,
12, 38, 59, 89, 104, 105, 111, 112,
139, 146–7
I.L.O. *Apartheid* Declaration and
Programme, 115–17
I.L.O. Conventions, 12, 89, 133, 146–
147
International Monetary Fund, 38, 74,
110
international organisations, legal
status of, 6–8, 45–9
International Slavery Convention,
145
International Telecommunications
Regulations, 12, 79
International Telecommunications
Union, 105, 110, 111
investment, 63, 75–6
Iranian Consortium, 49
Iranian tradition and the legal order,
42–3
Isidore of Seville, 127–8

Jackson, Andrew, 140
Japanese tradition and the legal order,
84–5, 98

John XXIII, Pope, 122, 128
judicial inquiry into facts, 10–11, 26–7, 70–1
judicial inquiry into policy, 155–6
judicial innovation, 44–5, 53–5, 81–7, 137–8
Justinian, 43

K'ang Yu Wei, 93
Kojhejnikov, F. J., 6
Koo, V. K. Wellington, 87
Korovin, E. A., 7

Lachs, Manfield, 30
las Casas, Bartolomé de, 127
law enforcement, 71–3
League of Nations, 14, 61, 68, 71, 73, 103, 113, 146
legal equality, 142–4
legislation, international, 11–13
Leibniz, G. W., 33, 128
Lenin, V. I., 34
Leon, Fray Luis de, 133
Lincoln, Abraham, 134, 139
Locarno Treaty, 32
Locke, John, 87, 128

Magna Carta, 36, 151
Mahomet, 88
Maine, Sir Henry, 66
Maitland, F. W., 107
Makino, Baron, 134
Marshall Plan, 75, 76
Marx, Karl, 32, 88
Mekong River Project, 76, 92
Mickiewicz, Adam, 30
Milton, John, 128
Mohammed Reza Pahlavi, H.M. Shah, 42, 53
monetary policy, 74–5, 80
multi-national corporations, 49–51
multi-racial societies, 135–7
Muslim attitude to law of nations, 88
Muslim tradition and the legal order, 86
mutual aid, 3, 66–82, 92

NATO, 35–6, 41
non-alignment, 61, 68–70
nuclear energy, 51–2, 64, 158
Nuclear Test Ban Treaty, 64, 158

objectivity, concept of, 25–8

Oppenheim, L. F., 6
Organisation for Economic Co-operation and Development, 38, 41, 75, 77
Organisation of African Unity, 36, 40, 107, 122
Organisation of American States, 36, 40, 107
Organisation of Petroleum Exporting Countries, 50
Ortega y Gasset, José, 140

Pacem in Terris, 122
peaceful change, 155–6
peaceful settlement, 26–7, 60–1, 154–5
Permanent Court of International Justice, 99
Plato, 31, 98
policy and morality, 56
political equality, 141–2
political matters, responsibility for in United Nations family, 109–12
Pollock, Sir Frederick, 32
private law, unification of, 72–3
private international law, 71–2
procedure, regularity of, 13, 114

regional arrangements, 21, 40–1
regularity of procedure, 13, 114
Rhodes, Cecil, 140
Roosevelt, Franklin D., 151

Sa'di, 53
Scelle, Georges, 34, 119
scientific and technological progress, 26–7, 39, 51–2, 63, 78–9, 158–9
Scott, James Brown, 119
Shotoku, Prince, 98
slavery, 145–6
social equality, 145–8
social justice, 38–9, 62–3, 125–6, 130
Socrates, 140
Sorel, Georges, 32
Southern Africa, 105–6
sovereignty, 5–6, 23–4, 31–41, 61, 129–31
space exploration, 13, 29–30, 51–2, 64, 78–9, 81
Spanish tradition and the legal order, 126–31
Spinoza, Baruch de, 128
Suarez, Francisco, 119, 127, 129, 130

subjects of international law, 6–8, 45–51

Tagore, Rabindranath, 65
Tanaka, Kotaru, 44, 87
territorial integrity, respect for, 90–1
third-party judgment, 35, 70
tolerance as legal obligation, 3, 83–5, 87–90
trade, 63, 77, 80
Treaty on Principles Governing the Activities of States in Space, 13, 29, 64, 79, 81, 158
Tunkin, Grigori, 2, 8, 30

Ulpian, 127
ultra-hazardous liability, 51–2, 81, 91
uncertainty in the law, 26, 98–9
United Nations, 21–2, 40, 103, 105, 108–10, 118
  Charter, 18–19, 21, 25, 36, 58, 60, 61, 62, 68–9, 70, 88, 89, 90, 91, 104, 109, 121, 134, 139, 153
  General Assembly, 12–13, 16, 27–8, 70, 132, 143, 156
  Security Council, 27, 70, 73, 81, 143
United Nations Codification Conferences, 12
United Nations Covenants on Human Rights, 2, 28, 29, 37, 62, 72, 88, 89, 121, 122, 126, 132, 134, 141, 143, 151, 157
United Nations Development Programme, 75, 76
United Nations Educational, Scientific and Cultural Organisation, 105, 110, 111
United Nations International Law Commission, 12, 43
United Nations Scientific Conference

on Application of Science and Technology to Economic Development, 80
United Nations Scientific Conference on Peaceful Uses of Atomic Energy, 80
United Nations Scientific Conference on Peaceful Uses of Outer Space, 81
United Nations Special Committee on Friendly Relations and Co-operation among States, 16
United Nations Trade and Development Conference, 22, 38, 40, 63, 77, 145, 156
Universal Declaration of Human Rights, 2, 28, 37, 72, 88, 89, 113, 121–6, 134, 141, 143, 151, 157
Universal Postal Union, 105, 110, 111
universality of world community, 13, 16–19, 106–9

Victoria, Queen, 138
Vinogradoff, Sir Paul, 66
Vitoria, Francisco de, 119, 127, 128, 129, 132
Voltaire, 128

Westlake, John, 7
Wilson, Woodrow, 69
Winiarski, Bohdan, 27
Wirtz, Willard, 135
World Health Organisation, 105, 107, 110, 111
World Meteorological Organisation, 79, 110, 111
World Rule of Law Centre, 24

Zimmern, Alfred, 134
Zoroaster, 42